THE MIDDLE GAME IN CHESS

Eugene A. Znosko-Borovsky

Translated by J. du Mont

D0064065

Dover Publications, Inc.
New York

PREFACE

A third edition of Znosko-Borovsky's pioneer work, *The Middle Game in Chess*, having been sold out, the question of a reprint became urgent.

An artist in the true sense of the word, the author was not satisfied with a mere reprint of the work as it stood, successful though that has been. Instead of this line of least resistance, he set out to write an entirely new book, in which the experience and concentrated thought of the last twelve years have found a happy expression.

The really outstanding positions from the old book have been retained, but treated in a manner far more concise and easy to comprehend.

At the same time, new and profound ideas are illustrated by positions from the very latest master practice.

True to the pioneer spirit, which is perhaps the most striking feature of the author's character, he gives his readers, in Chapter I of Part II, a lucid exposition of those bugbears of the average player, the transition stages between Opening and Middle Game and between Middle Game and End Game.

For the first time in the history of chess literature, this important subject finds adequate and authoritative treatment.

My thanks are due to my friends F. W. Allen and D. Castello for reading the proofs.

J. DU MONT

This Dover edition, first published in 1980, is a republication of the fourth, revised edition as published by David McKay Company in 1938. The main text is unabridged, but a two-page List of Illustrative Positions has been omitted.

International Standard Book Number: 0-486-23931-4
Library of Congress Catalog Card Number: 79-55840

Manufactured in the United States of America
Dover Publications, Inc.
180 Varick Street
New York, N.Y. 10014

CONTENTS

CONTENTS

PART I. GENERAL REMARKS

I. THE MATERIAL BASIS OF THE GAME

1. THE ELEMENTS

(a) Space

A GAME of chess is contested within a strictly geometrical space, namely, a square board sub-divided into 64 squares of equal size. There is no physical difference at all between any of these squares, their colour being only a matter of convenience, making them easier to survey.

Yet their respective location on the chessboard affects their individual importance. This distinction becomes evident when we compare the squares situated on the edge of the board with those in the centre. The centre squares are, for all practical purposes, at an equal distance from the corners of the board ; in consequence it is easy to support from there any point that may be attacked or, conversely, to initiate an attack wherever opportunity offers. In practice, whoever controls the centre has the command of the whole board.

The centre squares being surrounded by other squares, any piece posted there radiates power in every direction, whereas its effectiveness is considerably less if placed near the edge of the board, as there it lacks at least one side for its radiation ; in the corner it is even cut off from two sides.

The less radiation a piece possesses, the smaller is its power. Therefore pieces gain in strength by approaching the centre ; they are strongest when posted there.

Every piece has theoretically an absolute and constant value ; but in practice its effective value varies according to the square it occupies. It is therefore of very real advantage to obtain control of the centre.

It must not be assumed that the best tactical plan is to place all one's pieces in the centre, thus rendering them as powerful as possible. This would only lead to the forces facing four fronts instead of only one as in the initial position. In addition numerous pieces massed within a small space would obstruct each other and become less instead of more powerful. Finally, our task is not only to occupy strong squares, but equally to guard our own weak squares against intrusion by the enemy.

It may be said that the occupation of a centre square by placing a piece upon it is not always necessary : it is at times sufficient merely to control it, thereby preventing its occupation by a hostile unit. Actual occupation is only of value if it is more or less permanent.

Apart from the small centre of 4 squares, we can speak of a wider centre comprising the 16 squares nearest the middle of the chessboard.

One could while the time away by making a valuation of each square starting from the small centre, where the value is 36, down to the corners, where it dwindles to 23. These valuations, however, could at best be of interest to the mathematician ; the practical player only values ideas.

The lines which are formed by various sequences of squares can be divided into two main groups :

    I.   Vertical (files) and horizontal (ranks).
    II. Diagonals.

The last named have the distinctive feature that they

comprise squares of one colour only. For this reason a Bishop which moves diagonally cannot control the whole chessboard but only half of it : hence its limited power. Diagonals are of varying length : the longest comprises 8 squares, the shortest only 2. All other lines, vertical and horizontal, always contain the same number of squares, namely, 8.

From any square, in the centre or otherwise, there are always 14 squares on lines of the first group.

The maximum number of squares on diagonals, namely 13, is available from each of the 4 centre squares. This number is smaller the farther we get from the centre, the minimum being 7 from any outside square. We must therefore conclude that the diagonal is the weakest line on the chessboard. It is of practical importance to realize the strength of a diagonal which is about to be occupied. A line affects the power of a piece in the same way as does a square.

If the importance of a line necessarily depends on its length, it depends even more so on the part of the chessboard which it traverses. It is the strength of the squares of which it is composed which determines the value of a line. A line near the edge of the board has not the same importance as a line near the centre. We increase the power of our pieces by placing them on important lines, and therefore it is important to occupy such lines.

It is clear that the weakest lines are the outside ranks and files. But from a practical point of view the last ranks and files but one, forming the girdle Q Kt 2— K Kt 2—K Kt 7—Q Kt 7 must be considered the most vulnerable ; the reason is to be found in the fact that the outside ranks and files are protected on one side, so to speak, by the absence of further squares which makes them immune from a turning movement.

Ranks and files differ, in the main, in their direction. This distinction is of the greatest import, as in a normal game of chess there are only two adversaries.

As the forces are marshalled on horizontal lines, the front of each army is prepared to sustain and repel assaults on vertical lines, which are the lines of attack. Thus a number of ranks belong wholly to one camp or the other ; others provide the field of battle.

The case of the files is entirely different ; in each one of these there are squares which are in closer proximity than the others to one or the other of the players. Hence their character is diametrically opposed to that of the ranks. K 3 and K 6 are identical in every respect, but K 3 belongs to White and K 6 to Black. From the point of view of the players one is neutral, the other active. He protects the one whilst attacking the other. The file is active whilst the rank is neutral. With each square on a file activity goes on increasing, but on reaching the fifth we assume the initiative and start the attack with all the attending risks.

We cannot allow an enemy piece to settle down within our lines, as, for instance, on our third rank ; at the same time we try to occupy corresponding squares in the enemy's camp. It is of great advantage to us if one of our pieces, having reached such an advanced position, can be maintained there ; if it is driven back we have in most cases only wasted time.

Thus we perceive that in addition to the value of each square on an empty board, there is another and different valuation depending on the disposition of the two armies ; we shall see that further variations occur according to the relative position of the pieces at any given moment. As the squares influence the pieces, in the same way do the pieces affect the value of the squares, which value varies consequently with every move. We must acquire a clear perception of the difference between the constant and the variable value of the squares, which is of the utmost importance for the proper handling of a game of chess. It is easy enough to remember the first ; but it is far more difficult correctly to assess the changes which are constantly occurring. But if insufficient attention is given to this matter, and one adheres blindly to the constant and preconceived valuation, it will not be noticed in time when the usually strong and sound has become weak and precarious.

Although our chessboard is an ideal square—and the lines thereon are perfectly regular—this space in which the chess-men do battle is not altogether similar to spaces which we find in geometry or in everyday life. It is a strange world, subject to its own peculiar laws.

Supposing you wish to travel from K R 1 to K R 7, you will remember what you have been taught at school, namely, that the straight line is the shortest distance between two given points, and you will follow the R file and accomplish the journey in six moves. But if your King should choose to travel diagonally in a broken line K R 1—K 4—K R 7 he will also arrive at his destination in six moves. The number of squares is the deciding factor, not the length of the journey.

Geometrical theorems (such as the square of hypothenuse) are not valid on the chessboard. Take the right angle Q R 4—Q 4—Q 1, and you will see that each side Q R 4 to Q 4, Q 4—Q 1, and Q 1—Q R 4 comprises four squares.

The possibility of employing with the same degree of effectiveness lines visibly different in length is of great importance, for, in consequence, it becomes possible to aim at several points at the same time, which is the basis of numerous combinations.

Let us examine the following position (Diag. 1):

DIAGRAM 1

Study by Réti

Black has played ... P—R 4 ; how is it possible to reach this pawn ? It seems out of the question, as the white King is two squares behind. The game to all appearances is irrevocably lost. And yet it yields but a draw. It is unbelievable, yet it is so.

Instead of playing K—R 7, following up the pawn on the same file, White plays on the diagonal 1 K—Kt 7, P—R 5 ; 2 K—B 6. If now 2 ... P—R 6 ; 3 K—K 7 protecting his Q B P on the next move and queening it in two more moves. If instead 2 ... K—Kt 3 ; then 3 K—K 5, threatening 4 K—Q 6, again guarding his Q B P. Therefore 3 ... K × P ; after which 4 K—B 4, P—R 6 ; 5 K—Kt 3, intercepting the black pawn.

The diagonal enabled the white King to stop the hostile pawn, which he could not have done by pursuing it on the file, for on the diagonal he was approaching his own pawn.

In this study the importance of a diagonal is clearly demonstrated, but equally so, the importance of the centre, for from here both flanks can be threatened at the same time. In this way we qualify, to a certain extent, what was said about the weakness of a diagonal. At least in the case of the King and the Queen (which can move on a rank, a file or a diagonal), the diagonal in a way unites the characteristics of vertical and horizontal lines.

It is essential to become acquainted and perfectly familiar with these peculiarities of the chessboard. They possess not only theoretical interest, but practical importance as well. How many lost games have been due to ignorance of them ! How many more to their neglect !

DIAGRAM 2

White : Yates ; *Black :* Marshall
Carlsbad Tournament, 1929

They must become a player's second nature and emerge subconsciously whenever they are needed.

In the position shown in Diag. 2, White, instead of choosing the shortest way to win, namely, 1 Q—B 2, decided on another line of play which he deemed to be just as safe : 1 K—B 4, P—Kt 8 (Q) ; 2 Q × Q *ch*, K × Q ; 3 K—Kt 4.   Black's R P falls and White's B P cannot be stopped as the adverse King is not within the "square."

Great was White's surprise when Black, instead of the expected 3 ... K—B 7; played 3 ... K—Kt 7; occupying another diagonal from where he can reach the adverse B P, because White must lose a move capturing Black's R P, which otherwise, protected by its King at Kt 7, would reach the queening square.

A player cannot be expected at all times to think out the correct line of play : he must have the feeling for it. To that end the chessboard and all its peculiarities must be perfectly familiar to him and hold no secrets.   It would be a good thing if every amateur could, without sight of the board, visualise all its lines and angles with a clearness and precision that would enable him, without thinking, to determine the colour of every square and the rank, file and diagonal on which it is to be found.

(*b*) *Time*

It is no easy task to speak of things that are neither visible nor tangible.

As regards space, we have the chessboard, but time in reality represents but an idea and is, in theory, unlimited.   On the restricted space of the chessboard this leads to strange happenings.

If in chess the unit of space is the square, that of time is the move. As in the case of the squares, the moves are always equal, alternating with strict regularity between the two players. Yet in making a move it is possible to lose time, which might be of paramount importance. To lose a *tempo*, it is sufficient to take two moves in executing a manœuvre which could have been carried out in one. Advancing a piece and moving it back again also loses time. It is tantamount to losing a strong square and surrendering it to the opponent.

There is another distinction : some moves are voluntary, others are forced. If there is perfect freedom in the choice of move and a wide range to choose from, the stronger the moves are likely to be. If moves are compulsory, it is a sign of weakness both of the position and of the pieces. Starting from the initial position with a limited number of possible moves, the object of the mobilisation is to obtain different positions with an ever-increasing number of available moves. Whenever this number begins to grow less it is a sure sign that the position is deteriorating and that the pieces are becoming correspondingly less effective.

Although moves are equal in point of time, it is important that they should be made at the right moment. The same move, played at different times, has entirely different values. The order of the moves is of the utmost importance. Not unlike the lines formed by squares, we have series of moves.

Chess is not played move by move, but in well-considered series of moves, which should meet all requirements, namely, freedom for the player, constraint for the adversary; proper timing of each individual move; use of the maximum power of each piece at all times.

The more numerous the moves conceived as one series, the wider the range of their possible variations and the greater their effective strength. A move which initiates such a sequence of moves is the move of a master. If it leads to nothing it is of no value; you must be thankful if it does not ruin your game.

We must also pay attention to another point, namely, whether our moves are active or passive. A real offensive begins when our threats are ahead of the opponent's defensive measures.

A game of chess can, on broad lines, be divided into three main phases : the opening, the middle game, and the end game.

Our primary object is to enter upon the middle game, which is the very life of chess, without lagging behind our opponent. If we drift into a middle game without having developed the whole of our forces, our game will be dominated by the adversary and in consequence our pieces will be weaker than his, and their freedom of action will be restricted. As in actual warfare, faulty mobilisation can be put right but rarely, and then only with difficulty.

Whoever starts the middle game with an advance in development and with the command of the centre, has every reason to hope for ultimate success.

Success will come to him whose end game represents the realisation of what has been achieved in the middle game. It is here, above all, that the factor of time becomes paramount. Speed plays a decisive part, for it might turn a pawn into a Queen. In the middle game time has as much value as space.

(c) Force

Space and time are the conditions in which chess is played. The active element is force. Force reveals itself in space and time, combines the two in its movements, and is itself, for its effective application, conditioned by them.

We have established a unit of time and a unit of space. Is there equally a unit of force? If so, is that unit subordinate to a particular principle? Were the answer in the negative the game itself would lose in balance and its laws would become arbitrary.

In examining the pieces which represent the element of force in chess, we shall find this unit. These pieces, one and all, obey the same principle; they are alike in all essentials. There are, it is true, some strange variations: e.g., the King cannot be captured, for the game is lost when he cannot avoid capture; a pawn can be turned into a Queen. But the difference between the pieces rests in their particular ways of moving; it can be stated that therein lies the only distinction between them.

The power of any piece depends on its speed, or, in other words, its power to control or threaten a certain space in a certain time. The greater the space and the shorter the time, the greater the speed of the piece, and consequently its power.

Force, as applied to chessmen, is therefore expressed in terms of time and space. Could there be a more eloquent demonstration of the logical consistency which forms the basis of chess?

As we have seen, the unit of space is the square; that of time is the move. In the same way we have a unit of force, namely, the motion in one move from one square to the next. In principle this unit is the pawn, although allowance must be made for the pawn's peculiarities, namely, the initial double move, the capture on a diagonal, and queening.

As we have said, the real difference between the pieces lies in their respective speeds : and we find in chess a curious state of affairs which is peculiar to that game. If a piece attacks another, it is not the weaker but the stronger one which has to give way. A light ball will always be driven back by a heavier one. In warfare, also, a more heavily armed aeroplane will force a less fortunate opponent to retire.

Another of the pawn's peculiarities is that it cannot retreat and, as each side possesses eight pawns, they form an arm distinct from the other forces.

As a unit amongst the pieces, one could take the King which, in one move, can occupy any adjacent square ; the King's move is the forerunner of the moves of all other pieces which command files, ranks and diagonals in any direction. The moves of the strongest piece on the board, the Queen, are merely an extension of the moves of the King, the weakest piece in chess.

For their moves the pieces use only lines existing on the chessboard, and in their variety they remain strictly logical, the result of the evolution of the chess move in the course of many centuries of chess history. One could imagine in chess absurd and fantastic moves, independent of any set laws ; indeed such moves have been tried in the history of chess. But in the final form of the game the uniformity and logic of its moves cannot be doubted. The only piece which seems to have pre-served something fantastic in its gait is the Knight. But a closer analysis will show that the Knight's move is based on the same principles as those of other pieces.

We have seen the relationship between the moves of

the King and the Queen. The Queen's moves combine those of Rook and Bishop; in other words it covers all the lines on the chessboard, vertical, horizontal and diagonal.

Concerning the Knight's move, which at first sight appears to be entirely arbitrary, it is very interesting to note, upon reasoned examination, that it conforms to the general scheme of things. Nor will it be devoid of practical usefulness to recognise this fact.

Fig. A

If we examine Fig. A we shall see that the Rook's move there illustrated geometrically bisects the angle formed by the Knight's moves K 2—K B 4—K Kt 6— K R 8 and K 2—Q 4—Q B 6—Q Kt 8. Thus the similarity of the Knight to the other pieces is manifest, as is also the regularity of its move which, at stated intervals, passes through a full square, after cutting across two intervening squares. It thus becomes apparent that the Knight's move is not crooked at all : it can move in a straight line, any desired distance across the board.

Fig. B shows how the Bishop on the long diagonal bisects the angle formed by two Knights moving from Q R 1 to Q 7 and K B 4 respectively.

FIG. B

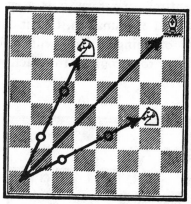

The two angles formed by the Bishop's move on the long diagonal from Q R 1 and the Rook's moves Q R 1 —Q R 8 and Q R 1—K R 1 respectively, are again sub-divided, although in this case not equally by the Knight's moves Q R 1—Q Kt 3—Q B 5—Q 7 and Q R 1—Q B 2—K 3—K Kt 4.

There can be no doubt that the Knight's move is closely related to the moves of all the other pieces and is based on similar principles.

2.   THE PIECES AND THEIR MANAGEMENT

There are in chess two distinct groups of forces, namely, the pawns and the pieces proper.

The pieces represent the dynamic element of the game whilst, normally, the pawns have a static tendency. Both have to fulfil different tasks according to their power and individual capacity.

(a) The pawns

The pawns differ from the pieces in two essential points : one is their weakness, or in other words their lack of speed, the other being their inability to retrace their steps.

Whereas the pieces can always return to a square which they were compelled to leave, a pawn, once started on its journey, can never turn back. For this reason a player must exercise the most extreme care in advancing his pawns. The eight pawns occupy all the files and show the enemy an unbroken front ; but once they are under way, their original front is left bare and allows the enemy to penetrate freely into the inner lines. Having once pierced the line of pawns, the opponent is no longer obliged to manœuvre vertically, as is the case in the initial position ; he can attack in all directions, which is extremely dangerous, as such attacks are the hardest to resist and to repel.

Therefore the pawns, used collectively, are the defensive force *par excellence*.

The rupture of their line or its disappearance, which is part of the opponent's plan, must have fatal consequences ; defence is therefore their first consideration.

To this end the best position for the pawns is the horizontal line, for in that case the whole of the rank in front of them is guarded, which renders any attack difficult to carry out. The pawns are in a position easily to protect each other : any pawn, which may be attacked, simply moves up one square. If, as in the case of the castled position, the King is behind the pawns, a pawn must be attacked twice before it is really threatened. On the other hand, any advance by pawns weakens the pawn position, and this for several reasons, of which the most important is that, if any pawn moves forward, two neighbouring squares are weakened, as they have permanently lost the protection of that pawn. These squares represent weaknesses which can be exploited by the enemy ; the most vulnerable point is a "hole", as for instance K Kt 3, when the pawns are placed at K B 3, K Kt 2 and K R 3. Pawns, when posted on the same rank, can easily evade most attacks by mutual protection, which is effected by a simple advance of one square by one of the pawns. On the other hand, a pawn, once advanced, leaves the pawn which is protecting it weak and backward, for that pawn cannot easily be protected by another.

If the pawn thus advanced is one of the King's field pawns (in the castled position) it becomes itself weak, as it is liable to be attacked : a pawn at K R 3 can be attacked in two moves by the hostile K Kt P.

Many and varied are the types of attack which can be made upon pawns. The object may be to create a weak square, or to weaken an advanced pawn, or to exploit the weakness of a backward pawn. For defensive purposes also it is of great importance properly to diagnose weaknesses in the pawn position, and to locate the most serious weakness both for attack and defence.

The disposition of pawns on a diagonal, where they protect one another, is also advantageous, provided the base of this chain of pawns is as far away as possible from the hostile forces. For it is the base which will be attacked, and if it is vulnerable, through being within striking distance, it may be possible to destroy it, causing the whole chain to crumble away. The same applies to a pawn-formation on two diagonals forming an angle. An attack against the peak of the chain can also become serious, as it may destroy a fortified outpost ; in the case of a "hill" formation on two diagonals (Q R 2, Q Kt 3, Q B 4, Q 5, K 4, K B 3, K Kt 2) the break-up of the peak destroys the whole lay-out and leaves two short pawn-chains. The greatest weakness, however, is the isolated pawn, particularly when doubled : protection by other pawns is permanently eliminated, and such pawns are at the mercy of enemy attacks. At the same time it is possible for a doubled pawn to have a high defensive value. Posted on an important file it commands the neighbouring squares and prevents the occupation of four valuable squares by hostile pieces, conversely securing these squares for its own pieces.

In addition, the doubling of a pawn opens a file which can be of the greatest value if it can be occupied by the Rooks ahead of the adversary. Nevertheless, the weakness of the doubled pawn remains ; we can only try to redeem it by gaining an advantage in another direction.

One of the distinctive features of chess is the combination of the various elements, which renders the game interesting and rather difficult ; for it is an art in itself correctly to assess advantages as against corresponding weaknesses. But in chess, we say it again, it is impossible, except against bad play, to have everything for nothing : a gain is nearly always attended by some loss of one kind or another. The question is which of the two is of greater moment.

Essentially a defensive unit, the pawn can, thanks in the main to its very weakness, become dangerous in attack. As it is an advantage to exchange a pawn for a piece, the pieces must retreat before an attack by pawns. The Queen may be as strong as eight pawns, but she must normally retreat when attacked by one of them.

When the pawns have started an advance, the opposing pieces must deem discretion the better part of valour and meekly retire. Such retreat must be decided upon as early as possible, lest the attacking pawns should gain too much time.

As soon as a pawn-attack can be foreseen, that part of the front should, as far as possible, be denuded of pieces. Then the pawns will only have the opposing pawns as the object of attack. Whilst this method is difficult and takes time, it will allow the defender to be thoroughly prepared. It happens but rarely that pawns can weaken the hostile pawn position, the forces on either side being similar in every respect. It is preferable to weaken the hostile pawn position by skilfully manœuvring the pieces, in order then to advance the pawns to the assault of the weakened position.

Such an assault can have varied objects. First of all, there is the break-through, the destruction of the enemy defences ; or else merely the occupation of weakened squares ; or it may be the opening-up of lines by means of pawn-sacrifices.

Owing to their small field of action, pawns are less suitable than pieces for the occupation of an opponent's weak squares. On the other hand, effective occupation by pawns is irrefutable and permanent : they are therefore particularly well fitted to *fix* a weakness, such as a backward pawn. A player who has a backward pawn will do his utmost to remedy the weakness ; the best means to that end is to advance it. This is best countered by placing a pawn in front of the backward pawn, making its advance impossible.

If it is important thus to fix a weakness, it is also necessary to blockade a strong pawn : the smaller the value of the blockader the better, and a pawn is indicated for the purpose.

A passed pawn, even if isolated, is of the greatest potential value, particularly if it is supported from the rear by a Rook, which helps its advance. With each advance of the pawn the field of action of the Rook widens and the freedom of the adverse pieces becomes more restricted. The precise moment when an isolated pawn (from being weak) becomes strong, is impossible to tell : here again it is a question of correct positional judgment.

It is not enough to know that centre squares are stronger than outlying ones, nor that a certain piece is more powerful than another : all that may change in the course of the game : according to the peculiarities of a position, normally strong squares may become weak, and weak pieces may acquire an unsuspected and abnormal accession of strength. If we do not make use of our opportunities, they will disappear, and a passed pawn, on which we had built our fortunes, becomes gradually a pitiful and helpless isolated pawn.

We must always recognise the weaknesses as well as the strong points in our position ; how they were brought about and how they can be reinforced. But it would be of little use merely to acknowledge that our position is inferior and to take the necessary steps to defend it : we must strive to the utmost to transform the position, so that its weakness may become strength. It depends to some extent on ourselves, when we have, for instance, a weak Knight against a strong Bishop, to alter the position in such a way that the Knight becomes more effective than the Bishop. Precisely in this consists the real struggle in chess.

(b) The King

There is little to be said about the King in a treatise on the middle game. Here the King is more or less inactive. In the end game, on the contrary, when only a few pieces are left on the board and mating threats are no longer to be feared, when even a pawn can become a Queen, then the King can and should take an active part in the struggle. In the middle game it is useless as well as bad tactics to expose the King to the dangers of the battle : his own weakness renders the King helpless when the opposing Queen goes berserk.

What can be expected of a King in the middle game ? Not to get in the way of his forces, and not to demand from them undue protection, which would diminish their offensive value. That is why castling generally happens early in the game : the King moves into safety, away from the strong squares (which will be the concern of other pieces) where he will no longer interrupt the *liaison* between the two Rooks. Generally speaking, castling on the K side will be preferable. It is the normal procedure, whereas castling on the Q side will generally have some special significance ; for in that case not only must the King make an additional move in order to get into real safety, but the Queen must have made a move, and castling on the Q side occurs therefore at a later stage. Under normal conditions castling K R is preferable.

Wherever the King is placed, the position in his vicinity becomes automatically weaker, for his presence attracts enemy attacks. If, in the same sector, the King were not present, an attack there would not have the same vigour, for the object of attack is naturally of less importance, as, for instance, the gain of a pawn. But

with the King there, a mate might be the result and, to
that end, no sacrifice could be too great.

However, in chess, a loss in one direction is seldom
unaccompanied by some gain in another ; in castling,
for instance, the King, placed behind his pawns, is
generally in no need of further protection from them.
Here he can play a definitely active role ; he might even
support their advance, or he can strengthen a hole
formed by the advance of a pawn, e.g., after P—K Kt 3,
the King can be posted at K Kt 2 and after P—K R 3,
he can move to K R 2 supporting the pawns thus
advanced and releasing a piece for some other important
duty. But it seldom happens that the protection of the
King's field by a piece can be dispensed with, and we
must decide which piece to employ for the purpose,
with the idea of limiting such protection to a strict
minimum. From this point of view a Kt at K B 3 or a
B at K Kt 2 are indicated, for not only do they protect
the King, but they are able to take an active part in the
game. A Knight at K B 1 is, defensively, quite as
effective as at K B 3, especially against a K side
attack, but it generally carries with it the drawback that
this Knight would remain entirely passive ; it would take
no active part in the operations, thereby demonstrating
the inferiority of the defender's position.

The mate implies the termination of the contest, but
a stalemate position is its prelude. The King must not be
allowed to remain in a stalemate position, that is, without
available moves, as then a check would spell destruction.
Only a born optimist would bank on his opponent being
unable to find a way, by means of unexpected sacrifices,
of inflicting this fatal check. Even a merely restricted
King's position should cause uneasiness when the squares

around the King are threatened by hostile pieces : therefore, in such cases, the opening up of files and, perhaps even more so, of diagonals, must at any cost be avoided.

We may begrudge the expenditure of forces in the defence of this feeble drone, but the safer his position, the more shall we be able to throw our available forces without misgivings into a decisive attack. Nor should we forget that, at a later stage, the King will come into his own and will himself decide the fate of the battle. He will then no longer be conscious of any inferiority and will act like any other piece, claiming space, occupying strong squares, and joining in the play in the centre. In the end game we must bring our King as quickly as possible into the centre of the board ; victory generally smiles upon him whose King is the first to arrive in the centre.

(c) *The other pieces*

Two of the pieces which remain to be analysed, the Rook and the Bishop, work on ranks and files, and diagonals respectively. In order to let them deploy their power to the full it becomes necessary to open lines for them. A Rook on a closed file is almost valueless, and frequently it is worth a sacrifice to allow this powerful unit to enter into the field of battle.

It is, however, not always easy to open a closed line, especially a file. The chessboard is so formed that the files lead to the hostile position and these files are occupied by our own pawns. The problem is then to eliminate one or other of these. If an adverse pawn or piece closes up a file, it is usually possible to exchange it, or to attack the obstructing unit with one of lesser value ; in the case of a hostile pawn, we can attack it with one of our own and force it to leave the file or be captured. But where one of our own pawns is in question, which, in addition, may be blockaded, the problem at times defies solution, and frequently only a sacrifice can achieve the desired end.

We must therefore always be on the look-out for a line that can be opened, always remembering that it must be an important one, that the opening of a line is of advantage to the stronger party, and that it should be where the player's position is strongest.

If the position there is endangered or if our position is inferior, it is better to keep it closed. What can be more alarming than to find that, after having gone to much trouble in opening a line, it has only benefited the adversary ! In opening a line, therefore, we must make sure that it will be to our own benefit.

But if the file in question is closed by our own passed pawn it is a different matter. The Rook behind it becomes extremely powerful ; under its protection the pawn advances irresistibly, and with every move of the pawn the Rook's field of action increases as does its power. The case of the Bishop is different : if the diagonal is closed by a passed pawn, this only hinders the Bishop : in advancing, the pawn loses the protection of the Bishop. The Bishop proves a poor defensive piece in such cases. The pawn may easily be lost but this is not always a drawback, as the Bishop, now liberated, is able to exert its full power, and this additional piece may decide the issue. In effect, for a pawn lost, perhaps against our will, we have gained the use of a Bishop—a favourable exchange.

As the opening of files for the Rooks is so troublesome one might ask whether it would not be better to place the Rooks in front of the pawns, thus avoiding the necessity for complicated manœuvres. Unfortunately, to post a Rook in front of the pawns exposes it to serious dangers : when attacked, the Rook, with its pawns behind it, would find it difficult to return to its own camp. The Bishop labours under no such difficulties : it is sufficient to advance a pawn in order to open a diagonal for it. If the B is at K Kt 3, P—K B 3 provides an easy retreat. The contrary obtains in the case of a Rook. Any pawn-advance would render its position still more precarious. On the same square K Kt 3, the Rook would only be worse off if a pawn were advanced to the same rank.

Another point to be remembered is that the power of the Rook is not increased by advancing it. A Rook at K 1 has the same power as a Rook at K 4. Here again the Bishop differs from the Rook in that its power increases as it advances ; not only that, but its effect changes in character. A Bishop at K 1 has no effect on the opposing camp, whereas from Q 4 it can attack both wings. At K Kt 2 the Bishop controls only the long diagonal, whereas from K 4 it commands two diagonals. It is therefore quite safe to place a Bishop in front of the pawns, the more so as, being of less value than the Rook, it has less to fear from enemy attacks.

Whilst the Rook, when posted on a strong square on a centre file, attacks the enemy centre, the Bishop can only do so from a flank. It is most effective, however, when on a strong square in the centre, attacking either flank, or, for instance, the castled King's position.

The Rook can exert its powers on the ranks as well as on the files, but it has but seldom an opportunity of doing so in the middle game. Within its own lines or in the centre, a Rook usually has little scope on a rank ; one or two pawn advances render it ineffective. Only a lateral attack on a rank within the enemy lines holds out promise of success. This refers particularly to the seventh rank. There the Rook attacks all the pawns, and if these have moved forwards, the King himself is in jeopardy.

Once a Rook is established on the seventh rank, it exerts its greatest power : the reason is to be found in the fact that the pawns act forward only, and therefore a pawn position is ill prepared to meet an attack coming from the flank. This explains also why the Rook gains in strength as the forces on the board begin to thin out towards the end game stage. The Rook is at its best when attacking the pawns in an end game ; it does great execution, where the Bishop, on the whole, cuts a poor figure. This can be explained by the fact that the lines of the Rook, the files and the ranks form an impassable barrier for the King or the pawns, whereas the Bishop's lines, the diagonals, can easily be crossed. A diagonal cannot block the King, but a rank or file stops him completely. In the middle game and on an open diagonal the Bishop is very powerful and, at times, the equal of a Rook ; but in the end game the Bishop, in order to be really strong, must have the help of the other Bishop. The two Bishops are then stronger than two Knights and they often hold their own against Rook and Bishop.

As a defensive piece in an end game, the Bishop is always stronger than a Knight, as it can stop a pawn at long range, which a Knight cannot do.

In order to illustrate the importance of lines in practical play, and the use which Rooks and Bishops can and should make of them, we give a position (Diag. 3) in which the critical square at White's K 3, the cutting point of the file K 1—K 8 and the diagonals K Kt 1—Q R 7 and Q B 1—K R 6, succumbs under the combined assault of Black's Queen, Rooks and Bishop.

DIAGRAM 3

White : Collins; *Black* : Znosko-Borovsky
Inter-club Tournament, Paris, 1937

With reference to the Knight we must first of all remember that it cannot control any lines. This weakness is often its strength, because it can exert its powers in positions in which other pieces cannot deploy theirs : the Knight is particularly at home in restricted positions with many pawns, which hinder the action of R and B, but cannot interfere with the Knight's unruly capers. The Knight should seek to occupy a strong square, if possible supported by a pawn, near the enemy lines. Unlike the Rook or the Bishop, the Knight can attack the enemy only by getting close to him : its best rank is the fifth. As the Knight acts in eight directions, it frequently happens that two or three of these directed towards the enemy are of practical use, whereas the Rook or Bishop usually have only one. Thus the Knight can attack the centre and the wing at the same time ; posted at K 5 it attacks Q B 6, Q 7, K B 7, K Kt 6. From K B 5 it would bear upon Q 6, K 7, K Kt 7, K R 6— all of them important squares. On account of its comparatively small value, the Knight only fears an attack by pawns and, for that reason, it is of all pieces the best adapted to provoke an advance by pawns : to prevent a Knight from establishing itself on the fifth rank, the adversary has often to take recourse to an otherwise perhaps undesirable pawn-advance (e.g., P—Kt 3 ; to prevent Kt—K B 5).

Placed in front of the pawns the Knight need not fear enemy attacks nor be concerned normally about possibilities of retirement ; but it must avoid the outside positions, where it is deprived of half its strength : at R 3 it has only four available squares and at R 1 only two. On a strong square in the centre, supported by a pawn, the Knight is frequently equal to a Rook. It is clearly superior to a Bishop provided the Bishop is of the colour opposite to that square.

As mentioned before, the Bishop is generally superior to a Knight in an end game. But with the hostile pawns placed on squares of the opposite colour, and therefore immune from attack by the Bishop, and with a Knight placed on a square equally immune, then the Bishop is of little value and the game is probably lost.

It may be added that, as a general rule, if the Bishop has little freedom, the Knight will have correspondingly more scope. It is then a matter of judgment to decide, for every position, which piece to preserve ; conversely, what kind of position you must seek to bring about to give scope to a certain piece.

To conclude, we shall say a few words about the Queen. There is not much to be said, as she combines the moves of both Rook and Bishop. It is only necessary to point out a few peculiarities in order to indicate the correct handling of the Queen.

Being able to move on a diagonal, the Queen, unlike the Rook, need not be afraid of moving into the open ; she can move with freedom outside the pawn-formation. But this must not be done too early, as in that case the Queen, lacking a real objective, might be harassed by the minor hostile pieces : nevertheless we must realise that the Queen's proper place, like the Knight's, is in front of the pawns in the centre of the board as her full power is available only in that position. From there the Queen is effective in three directions towards the enemy ; but it is necessary that the board should be, to an extent, denuded of forces. In the same way as an ocean-going ship, the Queen needs open spaces : narrow and restricted passages, where only a Knight can thrive, are not for her.

Posted away from the centre, the Queen acts only on a file or on a diagonal, which is obviously a waste of her power ; such a disposition would only poorly demonstrate our skill in fully employing the power inherent in our pieces.

We have so far spoken of the various chess pieces with reference to their moves : later we shall see their effect in various positions, and we shall learn how best to make use of their power and of their peculiarities.

3. The Co-ordination of the Elements as the Basis of Chess

The game of chess comprises three elements: force, time and space, and advantages in one or more of these decide the fate of the game. It is rare indeed for a player to have the advantage in all three elements and yet to fail in the end; such cases are exceptional. It is only to be expected that victory should depend on advantages obtained in these elements, and, whether we want it or not, every move brings with it some changes in them. We should see to it that these changes should be to our advantage. If we do not heed this fact, we could easily drift into a manifestly inferior position in spite of any brilliant ideas which we may have.

There are always outward signs which point to danger or to salvation: if we do not understand them or if we pay no heed to what they say, they will take their revenge: it is then that the mathematics and the logic of the game get their own back against abstract ideas.

It is desirable to have an advantage in all three elements: it creates a feeling of quiet confidence, which is favourable to the full use of our imagination. But, though this may be our aim, it happens but seldom. We may add here that such a sweeping advantage hardly ever obtains even in the moment of victory, when usually some decisive detail counts for more than the whole lay-out of the position.

The various elements are nearly always in a state of flux: an advantage in one element is, most likely, set off by a disadvantage in another. Their just appreciation is essential, for only then can we arrive at a proper valuation of a position and decide which side has the better game. To that end we must learn to distinguish advantages in each of the three elements.

This is not difficult in the case of force: the pieces are counted and whoever has more than the other has the advantage. If we have a Queen against a Knight our superiority is obvious. If we have a Rook for a Bishop we can also feel satisfied, unless, in either case, we have to deal with a sacrifice.

In the same way there is no difficulty in deciding which side is superior in space: whoever occupies all the important squares in the centre, commands the greater amount of territory, and the player can feel satisfied whose pieces have the greater freedom of action. It is almost an arithmetical sum and leaves as little room for argument: a simple calculation makes the real value of the position clear.

The essence of time is less obvious. In the opening it is still easy to perceive which side has developed better, but in the middle game, when the moves already made are a thing of the past and half forgotten, of what use is an advantage in time and how can we become aware of it ?

Yet here also a simple calculation can guide us. It is worth while to make it with special care: the more obscure an advantage in time, the more important is it to realise it.

If we examine the position in Diag. 4 we find that White has made 3 moves with his pawns, 2 with his Knights, 3 with his Bishops, 1 with the King (castling) or 9 moves in all. Against that Black has made 4 moves with his pawns, 3 with his Knights, 2 with his Bishops, 1 with the King (castling) and 1 with the Rook, in all 11 moves. In other words, Black has gained 2 moves.

A player who has such an advantage in one element would do well to realise it, and to try to improve on it, or at least not to lose ground in that respect, and to select his moves accordingly.

DIAGRAM 4

White : Capablanca; *Black :* Chajes
New York, 1913

If, on the contrary, a player is not conscious of this advantage, which is in fact something concrete and tangible, he runs the risk of its being frittered away and of seeing his position, from being slightly superior, changing to one of marked inferiority.

Let us examine the same game between Capablanca and Chajes 10 moves later and, to our amazement, we shall see that the position (Diag. 5) has undergone a radical change. In analysing the moves which have been played we shall easily ascertain that White has made 14 moves and Black only 12, White being thus 2 moves ahead after being 2 moves behind 10 moves earlier. In the last 10 moves he must in some way have gained 4 moves.

DIAGRAM 5

If it is easy to ascertain gains and losses in one particular element, it is at times exceedingly difficult to appreciate correctly the differences between the several elements, when there has been a gain in one of them and a loss in another.

In the case of "force," there is little difficulty for we know very well the value of the different pieces.

A gambit only means giving up material in exchange for rapid development; a sound sacrifice is one which brings about a sufficient advantage in another element; it is unsound when that advantage proves insufficient.

It would not be incorrect to say that a sound sacrifice is never a sacrifice at all. It is a very profitable exchange, or barter, much in the same way as trading with savages used to be in the early days: they were given glittering objects of no value in return for valuable commodities.

The same relation obtains between time and space and we can the better appreciate a position if we recall this fact.

As an example let us take the position in Diag. 6 after the 6th move of a French Defence, thus: 1 P—K 4, P—K 3; 2 P—Q 4, P—Q 4; 3 Kt—Q B 3, Kt—K B 3; 4 B—Kt 5, B—K 2; 5 P—K 5, K Kt—Q 2; 6 B × B, Q × B. We perceive at once that White has gained

DIAGRAM 6

space: is his position in consequence much superior? No one would assert that it is, otherwise this variation would no longer be adopted by Black. But Black has a compensating advantage in time, represented by one move.

It can be said that White has gained space but lost time, or that he has sacrificed time in order to gain space or, finally, that he has effected an exchange between the two elements. Whether the gain outweighs the loss it is difficult to say. Sometimes it is possible to find very clear indications as to whether it is so; sometimes it is a question of intuition and of positional judgment. But in any event it is essential to bear these things in mind and to realise their portent, for then a definite basis is given for the conduct of the game.

The main difficulty is, not so much to gauge the value of the advantages obtained, but to realize the fact that there are real advantages as well as those which are deceptive and spurious.

Suppose that we have advanced P—R 5; we have gained space without losing time, but this advance may have led to nothing and the pawn has become weak. Visible advantages are often a delusion. An analysis of actualities is clearly insufficient, although it is a necessity. It forms a basis for a deeper analysis to which we shall refer at a later stage. It must in fact be made with the most minute care, so that the true analysis shall be grounded on a really sound basis and not on positional judgment alone, which can frequently lead us astray and result in the worst errors.

For the moment let it suffice to draw the amateur's attention to the fact that the elements under discussion are not merely abstract and theoretical conceptions, but are in fact the very basis of chess, and that knowledge of them should be of great assistance in the conduct of a game.

II. IDEAS IN CHESS

The object of a game of chess is to administer checkmate. It happens but seldom that this can be effected in the early stages of a game. In order to enforce a mate it is often necessary to fight a fierce and frequently long-drawn-out battle. In the course of this contest we must proceed step by step, gradually increasing any advantage we may have, so that the mate occurs as the logical conclusion of our efforts. It would be futile to think of a mate the whole time, when at first no attack can threaten the adverse King. Against a strong player, or between well-matched opponents, it would be presumptuous in normal circumstances to expect to mate in, say, the first fifteen moves. Besides, it is of no importance whether it only happens on the 65th move, and whether it is effected by a raging Queen or a modest pawn, the last survivor on the board.

In our quest for superiority it is immaterial to us in which of the three elements it occurs. We must at times make prudent moves, whose sole object is to gain a *tempo* or the control of a strong square ; and we must not, without due care, capture a pawn left *en prise* by an astute adversary. But one must never forget that an advantage in one of the elements represents an advantage in position and, moreover, that it determines the character of the play; an advantage in space cannot be exploited in the same way as an advantage in time.

The game of chess, however, is not mechanical; the intellect predominates. It is a contest of ideas within the framework of time and space, in a chess sense.

In the 16th century Damiano advised chess-players never to make a move without some object. In order to play well, it is necessary to know what objects it is wise to pursue, and by what means they can be encompassed.

In the second part of this book we shall make an exhaustive study of the secrets of the middle game and we shall examine in greater detail both the objects in question and the means of attaining them peculiar to each type of position. At the moment we can only generalise, and without claiming to be exhaustive we shall make a general and succinct survey of the various positions.

Every plan in chess aims at obtaining some well-defined advantage. Where the positions are even, we try to upset the balance in our favour; if our position is inferior we try to equalise; when we are lost, we endeavour to set our opponent multifarious problems to render his task more difficult. In a superior position we still try to increase our advantage until it becomes decisive. But, whether we wish it or not, any advantage we gain refers to one of the three elements. We may win a pawn or immobilise a hostile piece; we may occupy a strong square or restrict our opponent to squares or lines of no importance; we may reach a desired goal ahead of our opponent. But in addition there are the sacrifices in which, in order to surmount an important obstacle, we give up everything else, and then it is possible to be in a state of inferiority in all three elements and yet to win the game.

It is both impossible and useless to enumerate all the means by which our objects can be attained—opening and closing of lines, interception, isolation or doubling of pawns. Let it suffice to recall here some of the more important and frequent cases.

(*i*) *The discovered check.* Some players are fond of giving check, no doubt taking as true somebody's tag, "Never miss a check, it might be mate." In order to be effective, a check must compel the adversary to make some valueless if not damaging move. A discovered check, on the other hand, is nearly always very dangerous. The piece which discovers the check in most cases finds some important point of attack. Only too often does it happen that a discovered check brings about an immediate decision. A well-known example occurs in Petroff's Defence: 1 P—K 4, P—K 4; 2 Kt—K B 3, Kt—K B 3; 3 Kt × P, Kt × P; 4 Q—K 2, Kt—K B 3; 5 Kt—B 6 *dis. ch*, and wins the Queen.

(*ii*) *The double check.* A double check is a rare occurrence; when it does happen it generally has tremendous power, for the double threat cannot be parried except by the flight of the threatened King. It is not to be wondered at, if such a check frequently decides the game. Here is a striking example: 1 P—K 4, P—K 4; 2 Kt—K B 3, Kt—Q B 3; 3 B—Kt 5, Kt—B 3; 4 Castles, P—Q 3; 5 P—Q 4, Kt × P; 6 P—Q 5, P—Q R 3; 7 B—Q 3, Kt—B 3; 8 P × Kt, P—K 5; 9 R—K 1, P—Q 4; 10 B—K 2, P × Kt; 11 P × Kt P, B × P; 12 B—Kt 5 *mate*.

The discovered as well as the double check can be foreseen, and there are usually ways and means of taking timely measures against it.

More insidious is the check occurring in the following short game: 1 P—K 4, P—Q B 3; 2 Kt—Q B 3,

P—Q 4; 3 Kt—B 3, P×P; 4 Kt×P, Kt—Q 2; 5 Q—K 2, K Kt—B 3; 6 Kt—Q 6 *mate*. This check is neither a double nor a discovered check, though it has the characteristics of both. Take away the K P and we have a double check. As it is, the K P is pinned, and the result is the same. The threat is less obvious and therefore more likely to succeed. Without the K P Black would have anticipated the double check; with the K P he did not trouble to look for a threat.

Incidentally, it may be added that a double check always is a discovered check. The reverse is not the case.

(*iii*) *The fork.* A fork is a simultaneous attack on two pieces; the simplest and most frequent fork is that effected by a pawn.

If one of the units attacked is the King, can we still speak of a fork or should we call it a double check ? In Asia, in former times, a simultaneous threat to the King and the Rook—which was then the most powerful piece—was called *shakrukh:* "check and Rook." It is a special and most decisive example of a fork. Here is an example culled from a chess-manual: 1 P—K 4, P—K 4; 2 Kt—K B 3, P—K B 3; 3 Kt × P, P × Kt; 4 Q—R 5 *ch*, P—Kt 3; 5 Q × K P *ch*, and wins the Rook.

The fork by a Knight provides a special case; no piece executes this manœuvre with the same amount of discretion and, one might be tempted to say, secrecy. When the Knight's fork is associated with a check, from a simple trap due to an oversight, it often leads to brilliant combinative play.

Examine the position in Diag. 7.

DIAGRAM 7

Study by Herbstman (1935)

Here White wins by means of a combination of great charm: 1 Q—K 1 *ch*, K—B 7; (1 ... K × Q; 2 Kt × B *ch*, followed by 3 Kt × Q.) 2 Q—B 1 *ch*, K—Kt 6; 3 Q—Kt 2 *ch*, K—B 5; (3 ... K—R 5; 4 Q—Kt 4 *ch*) 4 Q—Kt 4 *ch*, K—Q 4; 5 Q—Q 6 *ch*, K—B 5; 6 Q—B 5 *ch*, K—Kt 6; 7 Q—Kt 4 *ch*, K—B 7 (or R 7); 8 Q—Kt 2 *ch*, K × Q; 9 Kt × B *ch*, and 10 Kt × Q.

We see that the combination was based on the vulnerable position of the black Queen, where it is attacked by the Knight after Kt × B. The *modus operandi* was merely to force the black King on to any black square where it would be in check after Kt × B, thus effecting the fork. Incidentally, Black's King had to undertake a most pleasing circular tour !

(*iv*) *The pin.* The pin is a powerful means of tying up the adversary and of restricting the freedom of action of his pieces. A pin is effective only if the pinning piece is of less value than the masked piece, particularly if that piece does not protect the pinned piece.

If the masked piece is a Rook, it is good; if it is the

King it is best of all. The most favourable case is when
the pinned piece is insufficiently protected, for then all
the attacker's pieces will be brought to bear on it. In
all cases it is well to unpin the piece in question as
quickly as possible, not only to give it back its freedom
of action, but also to liberate the masked piece. Even
in the most innocuous case, where the pinned piece
enjoys sufficient protection, it is important to unpin it
so as to be able to use it freely; but it is essential to do
so whenever the pinned piece has only insufficient or
defective protection, as for instance in the most frequent
type of pin:—a B at K Kt 5 attacks a Knight at its K B 3,
protected by a pawn at K Kt 2, with a Q at Q 1 on the
same diagonal as the pinning Bishop. In order to avoid
the doubling of pawns the masked piece, the Queen,
must move away without giving up the protection of the
Knight, for instance, to her Q 3. The disadvantages of
a pin are often so serious that in many cases it is preferable to allow the doubling of pawns on the principle
that "of two evils, choose the lesser." The pinned piece
can be partially unpinned if we can interpose a Bishop
between that and the masked piece behind it.

However, one must bear in mind that, if the pinning
piece aims to some extent at the masked piece, it is
itself in danger. For instance, in the case described
above, if the pinned Knight can move away with a
check, the Bishop, if unguarded, can be captured by the
Queen. With a B interposed at K 2 as indicated above,
the case is even clearer: if the attacker plays a Knight to
Q 5 there follows ... Kt × Kt; and the pinning Bishop is
doubly attacked. Although a pin in itself is a straightforward and simple stratagem, this play and counter-play
between the pinning piece and the masked piece at times

gives rise to manœuvres of extreme subtlety and leads to the most interesting combinations, particularly when there is a double pin as in the following position (Diag. 7A): 1 ... R—Kt 7 *ch*; 2 R—Q 2, Q—Q 8; and wins.

DIAGRAM 7A

White: Travin; *Black:* Zeck
Leningrad, 1933

White's Rook at Q 2 is pinned at first by the black Rook, and afterwards by the black Queen also, and it is overwhelmed by the double task of guarding both its King and Queen.

After due allowance is made for possible risks, it must be said that a pinning piece is active, and it is always better to have active pieces rather than passive ones. In attacking a given point we obtain a certain advantage even if our opponent has sufficient forces available for its adequate defence, for all pieces thus employed will become passive and be deprived of their freedom of action, whereas, normally, our pieces will be able to discontinue the attack at any time according to our own free will and decision.

There are other means than these, more ruthless or more profound, of carrying on the attack; we shall have occasion to study them more exhaustively in Part II of this book. But they all belong to the category of threats and thus we must take cognizance of their nature at this stage.

2. THREATS

Nearly all manœuvres which we undertake in order to achieve our aims are in the nature of threats, and these threats at times may in themselves represent an object for which we strive. A threat is, at all events, the surest means of maintaining, if not of increasing, any advantage we may have, and that is why White, having the move, can always be the first to evolve threats, which should enable him to keep the initiative. To be sure, White has not an extra move; he has only a small part of a move—the right to make his move first. But it is sufficient to get ahead of the opponent; White is the first to threaten and Black has to defend, thereby losing some freedom of action, because his pieces will become passive and thus, to the slight advantage of the move will be added a greater, that of position.

There are innumerable possible threats; in order to study them more easily we must needs divide them into groups.

In the first place there are the direct threats by which the enemy is attacked at once, and then the distant or deferred threats, the effect of which becomes manifest only after a series of moves.

It is impossible to say which of the two kinds is the more powerful, and their effect varies. The immediate threat harasses the enemy and may deprive him of all freedom of action; the second, on the other hand, is less obvious, therefore more difficult to fathom. It requires time to evolve an adequate defence and it may be said that in general it is the more decisive and in any case the more dangerous of the two.

Let us examine the position in Diag. 8. White plays P—Kt 5, with the direct threat of capturing Black's B P and the more distant threat of winning the Queen, or

DIAGRAM 8

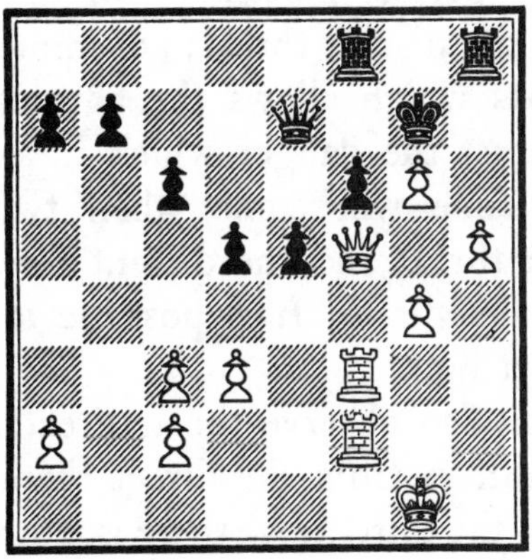

White: Tarrasch; *Black:* Janowski
Ostend, 1907

if the Queen moves away, of capturing one of the Rooks by 2 P × P *ch*, followed by P—Kt 7. Black easily parries the immediate threat by taking the pawn. But then White replies with 2 Q × R *ch*, R × Q; 3 R × R, exchanging the Queen for two Rooks, but maintaining the threat of winning Black's Queen by R—B 7 *ch*. If the Queen moves away there follows Q R—B 7 *ch*, and R—R 8 *mate*. Black is therefore compelled to give back the Queen by 3 ... Q × R; but if White were to take the Queen now, Black with two passed pawns against two passed pawns

can draw the game. But after 3 ... Q × R; White
plays 4 P—R 6 *ch*, and Black resigns after the following
continuation: 4 ... K—Kt 1; 5 P—R 7 *ch*, K—Kt 2;
6 R × Q, K × R; 7 P—R 8 (Q) *ch*. Thus the distant
threat has decided the game.

In this example we see a whole series of threats which
arise in turn without any respite. Black manages to
defend himself against each single, direct and immediate
threat, but succumbs in the end to the most distant
one. This is a perfect illustration of the best possible
exploitation of the distant threat: an uninterrupted chain
of direct threats which allows the adversary no leisure
to provide against the danger which lurks in the back-
ground. The time will come when two threats will
occur: a direct threat and the distant threat, which has
now become immediate. It is possible to parry one of
the two, but not both.

Here we can also observe the indirect though actual
threat, which differs from the direct threat in that it is
contingent. On the third move there is a threat of winning
the Queen—an immediate and direct threat; if the Queen
moves away there is the threat of a mate in two moves:
an indirect but immediate threat. This is an example of
a double threat: but an indirect threat can also occur by
itself, unaccompanied by a direct threat. For instance,
in the Cambridge Springs variation of the Queen's
Gambit Declined, Black's ... Q—R 4; contains no
direct threat, but it indirectly threatens White's Q B at
its K Kt 5.

Being less obvious than the direct, the indirect
threats are more dangerous: but as they are less forcible,
being themselves contingent only, there is nearly always
a choice of means in evading them.

Another group of threats contains real and sham threats; those which are a real menace to the opponent and those which only appear as such.

It may seem strange that a move which threatens nothing in reality can be called a threat and be taken seriously. It is a perfectly true saying that a threat is often stronger than its execution. An insignificant threat which persists for a certain length of time and burdens our play, forces us to bear it in mind, and to try to guess at what precise moment the enemy will choose to set it in motion. It is useless to insist that the threat is not serious, that it is a sham: circumstances may change, and very suddenly the same threat becomes acute and most embarrassing.

Already in the opening we have to deal with similar cases. Kt—K B 3 is not really meant to threaten the capture of the opposing K P, but should we carelessly overlook it at any time, we lose our K P. In the Ruy Lopez 3 B—Kt 5, does not actually threaten to win Black's King's pawn, but here again it may happen that a moment's inattention in the course of operations will cost us the K P, or at least cause us much trouble in winning it back.

The middle game provides more complicated examples: let us examine the position in Diag. 9. Here, as is well known, Black's normal development is ... P—B 4; which is very awkward for White because he has castled on the Q side.

If, however, this move is made without any preparation, it might lead to trouble for Black as follows: 1 ... P—B 4; 2 P × P, and if 2 ... Q Kt × P; 3 Kt × P, B × Kt; 4 B—Q B 4. But in order to make this variation possible the capture of White's B by a check must be prevented;

therefore White's first move must be K—Kt 1, a waiting move and a wise precaution against Black's ... R—B 1; and ... P—B 4. If now Black were to play 1 ... P—B 4; at once, he would, after 2 P × P, have to recapture the P

DIAGRAM 9

White: Rubinstein; *Black:* Znosko-Borovsky
St. Petersburg, 1909

with his Kt P. But then the continuation would be: 3 P × P, P × P; 4 Kt × Kt, B P × Kt; 5 B × P, P × B; 6 Q—Kt 3 *ch*, K—R 1; 7 Q × B, P × Kt; 8 R × Kt. It follows that Black must provide against White's 6 Q—Kt 3 *ch*, before he can play 1 ... P—B 4. White, by his preventive move, has avoided his adversary's real threat and rendered it inoperative; the fact that Black omitted the preparatory 1 ... K—R 1; has transformed into a real and serious danger what was originally a fictitious threat.

This position illustrates the play of threats and counter-threats which here is subtle and deep.

It frequently happens that fictitious threats have only a psychological object, that of intimidating a nervous opponent, who loses faith in his own legitimate threats in his anxiety about his adversary's imaginary menaces. This type of play is, however, abhorrent and contrary to the spirit of chess.

Let us imagine that, in the same position, Black has a pawn at K R 3 instead of K R 2. It is clear that he cannot capture White's Bishop as the open K R file would be far too dangerous for him. White can therefore leave his Bishop *en prise* in perfect safety. It is easy to imagine how, after a few moves, circumstances could have changed so that the Bishop, if still *en prise*, could in fact be captured; a fictitious threat has changed, under our eyes, into a real one. Lack of due attention has meant the loss of a Bishop.

It is impossible to enumerate all possible threats, from the simple to the complicated, from the ruthless capture of a Queen to the subtle occupation of a square or the contest for the centre. They all aim at one and the same object, the reduction of the opponent's freedom of action; they serve to restrict his pieces, to create weaknesses in his position, and to prevent him from occupying strong squares and open lines, while allowing us to do so ourselves to our own advantage.

III. STRATEGY AND TACTICS

1. Preliminary and Inner Analysis of a Position

We have seen that the analysis of the structure of a position is not sufficient for its thorough understanding. Yet it is an essential requirement and must be attended to with extreme care. Without it an analysis in depth is far more difficult and many important details might escape our attention; in addition, this preliminary analysis presents us with a general impression of the position, which either gives us confidence or creates alarm; in either case we know where we are. We must not overlook the fact that in making this analysis we learn to estimate a position integrally, and, after doing this very frequently, we shall learn to realise very quickly the exact value of any position. Take the position in Diag. 10.

It is easy to count up the pieces, the squares and the moves and to realise that White has the advantage in all

DIAGRAM 10

White: Leonhardt; *Black:* Marshall

three elements. He has an extra pawn, occupies the centre with his pawns at Q 5 and K B 4 and the Q at Q 4, and is a move ahead in his development (8 moves against 7). He has every reason, therefore, to be satisfied with his position and even before making the necessary supplementary analysis he can anticipate victory.

But, in chess, matters are rarely so simple and clearcut: the combination of the elements comes into play, and it is of far more frequent occurrence that an advantage in one element is set off by a disadvantage in another.

The position in Diag. 11 will convince us of this. With an equal number of pawns and pieces Black has evidently an advantage in space, thanks to his advanced pawns at K 5 and K B 4, and the Kt at K 4. But if we count up the moves we shall find that White has made 14 moves and Black only 11. Consequently, White is three moves ahead and it becomes necessary to weigh up the true value of the respective gains and

DIAGRAM 11

White: Vergani; *Black:* Teichmann
Hastings, 1895

losses in the different elements. These may balance each other, but it is also likely that the gains on one side are of decisive importance, whilst the opponent's gains, important in themselves, have little bearing on the actual situation.

It is easy enough to assert that the feeling for position, that mysterious instinct which the Germans call "*Positionsgefühl*" ("instinct for position" hardly does this word justice), is the sole arbiter in this matter and that there is nothing to be done for the player who does not possess it. We must not belittle the part played in chess by this instinctive feeling: it would be tantamount to belittling talent. But who is there who would maintain that, because this instinct plays a big part in the art of combination, the exact analysis of variations is superfluous or even impossible ?

The more complicated the position, the greater the part played by this positional instinct, which at times seems to discover that which one would hardly suspect to be there. On the smallest details, to which another would hardly give a thought, the lucky possessor of this "instinct for position" manages to build up an imposing strategic plan: on the *tout ensemble* of a position, without at times being able to explain why, he constructs a line of play which, after a number of moves, raises problems, the existence of which would never even have occurred to his less gifted opponent.

Nevertheless, can it be asserted that these hidden problems were not inherent in the position ? That hard facts have no part in it ? Is it not rather the case that the average amateur is content with a cursory and superficial appreciation of a position, so that important points are apt to escape his attention ? We shall refrain from answering this question, but shall, instead, strongly assert that it is worth while making a systematic attempt. This has never been done. But to cultivate the habit of analysis, in our sense, is the only way, not only of developing a correct appreciation of positions, but of creating that "instinct for position" in those who do not possess it.

Let us take our analysis a step further. Taking the same Diag. 11 (p. 49), a glance is sufficient for us to realise that Black has the advantage. How is it, then, that White has an advantage in time? Is it real or imaginary? How can we ascertain that?

First of all we can discern a number of pawn moves which are of little account, although in point of time there is no difference between them and moves of real significance. Two pawns have moved forward on the Q side, which is really passive in this position; there has been an advance by the K R P, which advance contributes nothing to White's development; finally, his K P has advanced one square only, by which the centre has been given up to Black, although, again in point of time, this move counts as much as a double move. The same applies to the pieces. The Knight has taken two moves to reach a most unfavourable square, which leads practically nowhere. The Q B has taken two moves in occupying a diagonal, which it could have reached in one, and where it more or less plays the part of a pawn in preventing the loss of the exchange. The second Bishop has made a modest move: it is posted on two diagonals, of which one is blocked by its own pawn whilst the other aims at nothing.

Thus it is quite simple to establish the fact that in reality White has no advantage in time at all, and that Black is the better developed. A very little time and thought is often all that is required to estimate correctly such gains and losses. But this analysis does not go as deeply as is necessary: it still is external analysis only, although a little more thorough. It would be a mistake to let it go at that, for, in order to play a game properly, it is necessary to grasp all the characteristics of a position down to the smallest detail, and a general survey such as indicated above would fall far short of what is required. When what we might call the inner analysis has been carried out conscientiously, we can proceed to the third phase of the complete analysis, namely, the individual analysis: the particular points which characterise a given position.

The structural analysis of the position in Diag. 12 shows equality of forces and of space, and a slight advantage in time for White (one *tempo*). Deeper analysis will lead to a very different valuation and will show that White has a great advantage.

DIAGRAM 12

White: Charousek; *Black:* Süchting
Berlin, 1897

The first fact which would strike the observer is that all the white pieces are developed, whereas two of Black's pieces are still on their initial squares; it would require at least three *tempi* to bring them out. The position of the remaining black pieces is equally unfavourable: the K R is blocked by an advanced white pawn, the K B is occupied in guarding a pawn, the Queen has no move, a Knight shuts in the Q B; only the Knight at Q B 3 is well placed, attacking a white pawn and defending its own, although it must be said that White's Knight is counterbalancing its effect.

By comparison White's development of his pieces is far superior. Both his Rooks are well placed, one of them protecting an advanced pawn and the other commanding an open file. Both Knights occupy excellent posts, even the one at Q Kt 3—normally an indifferent square for a Knight—for here it attacks Black's advanced passed pawn. Moreover it controls Q R 5 and Q B 5 and limits the action of the opponent's units, where he would be most likely to seek relief. The Bishops are even better placed: the K B at Q 3 stands on two open diagonals, the more important aiming at the opposing King's field; the Q B is blocked by its own pawn on one of its diagonals, but its influence is felt beyond that pawn. For instance, Black's Q cannot move to Q B 2 nor the Q R to Kt 1 because of the threat of P—K 6, at a propitious moment. Incidentally, it controls K Kt 5, a useful square in a K side attack to which the K B already contributes from Q 3. The Queen is passive for the moment; she completes the occupation of the centre files and disposes of two semi-open diagonals of which one is particularly important in case of a K side attack.

In the course of this structural analysis we have thrice

mentioned the possibility of a King's side attack. This tends to prove that such a simple analysis can give birth to a possible plan of campaign.

We shall later on see how such an idea must be elucidated, in order to decide on how to execute it. For the moment let it suffice to say that the position of the white pieces is such that a K side attack is justified and that a glance at Black's position shows that the King's side is denuded of defending pieces; therefore the situation is ripe for an attack on that wing.

Let us go back to our analysis. White's advantage in time is obvious, but it is also easy to discern his preponderance in space: it is necessary only to see which of the players controls the most important squares. To sum up: White's enormous advantage in position is undoubted, and one could even say that, thanks to Black's two undeveloped pieces, he has an advantage in force as well.

One point, however, remains to be cleared up: the comparative value of the two centre pawns, namely, White's K P and Black's Q P. They both have points in common and have a similar influence on the play of the pieces.

Black's Q P has the great advantage of being a passed pawn, whereas White's K P is impeded by the black K B P. On the other hand, unlike its counterpart, it is not isolated. This denotes a certain weakness in Black's Q P, which, however, can become strong if further advanced. The positional difference between the two pawns is more striking still. The K P attacks two important squares within the enemy camp, of which one (Black's Q 3) is unprotected by a pawn and thus can easily be occupied by White; the other square (Black's

K B 3) is even more important, being an essential square in the defence of the King's field—yet another portent. The two squares attacked by the Q P have not the same importance as they are both guarded by white pawns. The K P cannot advance because of the K B P, and, similarly, the Q P is blocked by the K B, which at the same time remains very active. Finally, if we add that the K P is in close proximity to the active K side, whereas the Q P is next to the passive Q side, there is no more to be said on the subject.

Thus, having carefully analysed the position, its possibilities have become much clearer to us. Are we now able to decide what to do ? Can we say that we are no longer in the position of a player who knows that he has the advantage, but is at a loss how to exploit it ?

In order to arrive at a final solution of the problem, we must end up with what we might call an individual analysis, which is nothing else but a careful analysis concentrated on one or two particular points from which the position derives its character.

The characteristics were revealed by the deeper analysis, and the three main points were: two undeveloped black pieces, the relative value of the opposing centre pawns, and the possibility of a direct K side attack. The first point tells us that it would be unwise to delay matters, for if we give the adversary sufficient time, he will develop the pieces in question, for which he only requires two moves.

The other two points indicate the line of play which must be followed.

Which of the two centre pawns is the weaker; which one is being, or can be, effectively attacked ? Black cannot very well give the matter much thought until he has completed his development; were it Black's move he could at once play ... B—B 2; attacking the K P whilst giving up his own Q P. Still more logical would· be Kt—B 1—Kt 3, after which Black's position would be satisfactory. But it requires time.

Against this, White can with advantage attack the Q P by retreating the Bishop. But it must not be overlooked that, should he simply retire the Bishop to Kt 1, Black can reply with Kt—B 1;—a useful move against a poor one, whereby the Q P is now guarded by the Queen; Black then pins the K Kt by B—Kt 5; and is out of his difficulties; he has even brought out his two undeveloped pieces. It follows that White's attack on the Q P must be accompanied by a threat. The move B—Q Kt 5, is indicated; not only is the Q P attacked three times, but one of the supporting Knights is under fire as well, and remains pinned if the other Knight moves away. Thus the Q P falls and the positional advantage turns into an advantage in material.

However, there are certain objections. Black will simply abandon his Q P, opening a diagonal for his K B. He then remains with two Bishops, the Q B occupying the long diagonal, with the threat of a possible K side attack. In default of anything better, this result might be acceptable to White, but one may well ask whether his positional advantage is not too substantial to be exchanged for such a small gain in material?

The idea of a King's side attack follows quite naturally. All is ready for a Bishop's sacrifice at K R 7; the essential pieces are available and there is no defending Knight at Black's K B 3 or K B 1. But after B × P *ch*, K × B; Kt—Kt 5 *ch*, K—Kt 1; Q—R 5, Kt—B 1; Q × P *ch*, K—R 1; White cannot bring his Rooks into play as Black's Q P prevents them from occupying the third rank, nor has the Knight sufficient time to move up and effect a mate.

Another point must be considered: Black's King could seek refuge at K Kt 3. Again this combination might turn out to be satisfactory for White, as he remains with two pawns for a piece and a strong attack.

We must now ask ourselves, in view of the fact that this continuation also is unclear, whether there is not another means of exploiting White's positional advantage—not, however, by lengthy preparations such as bringing up the Knight or advancing the K side pawns, for then Black would have time enough to complete his development. Having an advantage in time White would thereby offend against one of the basic principles in such positions. It is essential to proceed by way of threats. Automatically the move Kt—Kt 5, suggests itself. If ... P—K R 3; is played, Q—R 5, wins easily, as does P—K 6, in reply to ... P—Kt 3. Finally, after ... Kt—B 1; the continuation Q—R 5, P—Kt 3; Q—R 6, threatening Kt—K 4, and Kt—B 6, or Kt—Q 6, is very troublesome for Black.

The only drawback in playing Kt—Kt 5, lies in the fact that it leaves the K P unguarded, and Black will at once take advantage of it by playing K Kt × P; opening the diagonal for the Q B. There follows: 2 Q—R 5, P—K R 3; 3 B—R 7 *ch*, K—B 1; (... K—R 1; 4 Kt × P *ch*, Kt × Kt; 5 B—Kt 6,) 4 B—K 4, B—Kt 5; 5 Q—R 4, P × Kt; 6 Q—R 8 *ch*, K—K 2; 7 B × P *ch*, K—Q 2; 8 Q × P, and wins.

We need not, at this juncture, seek to decide which of the three continuations (B—Q Kt 5, attacking the Q P, B × P *ch*, or Kt—Kt 5, King's side attack) is the soundest and the most decisive (in the actual game Kt—Kt 5, was played); it is sufficient to establish the fact that the complete analysis, working step by step from the externals to the deeper characteristics of the position, allows us to realise the inward significance of the situation, thus indicating what aims to pursue.

It may be said that these could be perceived without the help of this analysis; if so, it could only be because they are sufficiently obvious. But this is the case in but few positions; in all other cases this type of analysis becomes invaluable. It is hardly possible that, after carefully examining the potentialities of each piece one by one in something of the same manner as we have done here, we should not become aware of the basic ideas inherent in a position. We necessarily must see with the utmost clearness the advantages or disadvantages which obtain, the characteristic lines of the play and how clearly they are defined. On that will depend the degree of intensity of our play; it will even determine the proper direction of our attack. More is not needed.

2.   The Position as a Whole

We have said that cases rarely occur in which all the advantages of time, space and force are to be found on one side whilst the general and real advantage is on the opposing side.

See, for example, the position in Diag. 13.

Black has two extra pawns. Even if he loses the K P he will still have a majority of one pawn. He has 14 moves to his credit against 10 by his opponent; thus he has

DIAGRAM 13

White: Morphy; *Black:* McConnell
New Orleans, 1849

gained four moves. Finally he has more space, thanks
to his advanced K side pawns, with a pawn on the sixth
rank, which advantage will be slightly counterbalanced
by the loss of his K P. And yet, in spite of all these
advantages, Black's game is manifestly inferior, and he
resigned after a few moves. The strength of the position
as a whole is decisive here, and this is not a question of
an automatic adding up of the various separate elements.
Once we have made an analysis of a position we must
know how to complete it by synthesis.

Two points here are particularly noticeable. The first
is the concentrated action of the forces. A piece may
occupy a strong square and yet have no prospects and
lack all effective force. Worse still, it may have power
and yet be of no assistance whatever to the other pieces.
It is then sheer dead weight. If you have an extremely
well-placed Knight at Q B 3, but you are engaged upon
a K side attack, the Knight will be of little use to you.

You may be ahead both in space and in time, but if your adversary's pieces are available for the defence of the attacked K side, you play with one piece less and your attack is doomed to failure. Most sacrifices are based on such circumstances: you give up a piece, or even two, because the opponent has not yet developed some of his pieces or is unable to bring them to the threatened quarter.

The second point, the logical complement of the first, is that, in the middle game, when a certain plan is under consideration, the general principles (occupation of the centre, open lines, strong and weak squares) are of less account than the selection of an object of attack, against which all the available forces are to be launched. On this point Alekhine goes so far as to say "all general considerations must be entirely forgotten" and "only that which contributes to the execution of the plan selected is of any avail."

In this statement, in itself so general and categorical, there is a certain amount of exaggeration. If we disregard the very foundation of reasoned strategy, retribution is bound to overtake us. An attack, successful in itself, may be compromised by an inferior pawn position. Again, it is well known that a flank attack is best parried by a thrust in the centre ; if the centre is neglected a seemingly winning attack turns into disaster.

At the same time it is true that all these "first principles" need not at all times dominate our play. You cannot conceive a plan, commence an attack, and look backwards all the time. Every decision contains a certain risk; if all risks are to be eliminated it is best not to play chess at all; we should be a beaten foe from the very beginning, for all our moves would be timid and spineless. "*Fortes fortuna juvat.*"

In judging a position as a whole, it is necessary to realise whether there is a point of attack which is decisive for the whole game: should there be one, then is the time to concentrate the whole of the forces, leaving all unimportant points bare of troops. The alternative, play over the whole board, necessitates a judicious distribution of forces and leads to a game both more difficult and more complicated. The first-mentioned type of position leads to rapid combinatory play, the second is typical of positional play with its numerous and slow manœuvres. When the ultimate aim of the game, namely, the mate, is within sight, then the utmost boldness is warranted.

3. CONSTRUCTION AND EXECUTION OF THE PLAN

In the foregoing chapters we have seen all the fundamental ideas on which the elaboration of a plan can be based. There are two points which must, however, be borne in mind. It must not be thought that a plan will occur to us fully worked out in all its details at a given moment, like Pallas Athene arising fully armed from the head of Zeus. Step by step, after the tentative manœuvres of the opening, it takes shape in our mind, at first in vague outlines, gaining gradually in definition and character. Where the position is simple and the advantage well defined, there is no difficulty in formulating at once a suitable strategic plan. But it is not possible to do this at will in obscure and complicated positions of no definite character, where both sides have equal chances, or, worse still, where the formations are symmetrical. It must then suffice to evolve an idea, without realising quite how to carry it out, or even where it will lead.

Secondly, let it not be imagined that one single plan is all that will be required in the course of a whole game. Even the most general strategic plan, based on wide conceptions, cannot embrace all the varied phases of a game. It may possibly happen that a single idea may form the basis of a game of chess, if this game be not too long, and of fairly uniform simplicity. But usually more or less clear-cut plans follow one another, covering series of moves more or less extended. It is not only that the human brain can hardly conceive a whole game, even a short one of only thirty moves, or that the opponent's resistance may be of a strength and variety impossible to foresee, but first and foremost that the average plan hardly ever brings about an immediately decisive result.

Having achieved an early object and scored a point, we perceive that the road to victory is still a long one, and that there will be further objects to be decided on and attained. And what devious ways will have to be followed ! At one time the opponent will try to lure us from our path by a tempting bait, at other times his mistake will tempt us to abandon our strategic idea in favour of an immediate and real tactical advantage. Or again, his tenacious resistance takes away all that made our object a tempting one and forces us to seek other aims. A game of chess is often not just one single battle, but a whole campaign. We get the worst of it at one point, but prevail at another; a whole series of battles is fought on the chessboard in the space of a dozen moves or so.

Though it may happen that a guiding idea recurs

constantly and at intervals like a *leit-motiv*—and such games often are of classical beauty—it would be wrong to make it a rule; it would only be detrimental to our game, built upon logic and imagination, and rich, above all, in possibilities and in variety.

Yet, bearing all this in mind, it is impossible to play a satisfactory game without following a strategic plan, which sooner or later will have to be evolved. To settle on a plan too late means an advantage to the opponent, who will be ahead of us in his threats; to have no plan at all would render our play inconsistent—without logic and therefore without strength.

Let us examine a position (Diag. 14) which is comparatively simple and in which the object pursued is of

DIAGRAM 14

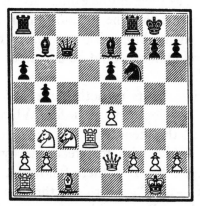

White: Lasker; *Black:* Capablanca
Match, 1921

a restricted nature. This renders the elaboration of a plan considerably easier, an important point in the preliminary examination of the position.

The games are approximately even, being equal in

force and space, with, however, this rather strange circumstance, which gives food for thought, that, although White has a K P on the fourth rank whereas Black's K P is at its third, Black has the control of the greater number of centre squares. Another unusual point, which is revealed by the analysis of the element of time, is that White, who has an advantage of one move (9 against 8), has not yet developed all his pieces whilst all of Black's pieces are in play or readily available.

Getting down to details, we observe that White's Q B is still on its original square, impeding the Q R; we notice also the strange position of the K R on the third rank, and the bad position of a Knight at Q Kt 3, whilst the other Knight at Q B 3, usually a good square for a Knight, is under the impending threat of ... P—Kt 5; a serious threat as the Knight would have no good square available. Against this the position of all Black's forces is extremely favourable; with two more moves by the Rooks his development would be completed and superior by far to White's.

The essential objects of both players are for Black to complete his development, and for White to save his K P which is threatened by the advance of Black's Q Kt P. If White tries to effect this by the simplest means, namely, 1 P—B 3, there follows: 1 ... P—Kt 5; 2 Kt—Q 1, P—Q R 4 ; with the threat of ... B—R 3. At present nearly all the white pieces are badly placed. Let us try another way : 1 P—Q R 3, P—Q R 4 ; 2 Kt × Kt P, Q—Kt 3 ; winning the K P. There remains only the advance 1 P—K 5. This opens the long diagonal, and now the white K Kt P will be under fire from Black's Q and Q B. The threat of a Bishop at Q B 4 will prevent the defensive P—B 3, by

White. How is this future menace to be parried ? We see that the problem has changed even before the first move is decided upon. The reason is that it would be too late to seek a remedy after we have committed our-selves to a certain line of play; eventualities must be foreseen and weighed up.

Our Rook at Q 3 can now render valuable service by moving to K Kt 3, where it protects the K Kt P and, in addition, enables the backward Q B to develop at K R 6 without loss of time. This is a rule of general applica-tion: if a piece is badly placed, before withdrawing it with the loss of an important *tempo*, one must seek to extract some advantage from its supposedly unfavourable position. In this case, why not assume that the Rook was placed at Q 3 in anticipation of some action on the K side ?

Thus does White's first plan take shape—advance of the K P, followed by R—Kt 3, and B—R 6, which move completes his development. It is easy to see that Black's ... P—Kt 3; would not hinder this plan in the least. White's Bishop could still go to K R 6, and in addition there would be a most desirable square for a white Knight at K B 6.

Without examining Black's point of view in detail, let us see how this plan of White's would work out.

After 1 P—K 5, Kt—Q 4; 2 R—Kt 3, Black plays 2 ... Kt × Kt; forcing the recapture by the Rook which must leave its post of attack: 3 R × Kt, Q—Q 2 ; now White reverts to his original plan by 4 R—Kt 3, and Black plays first of all 4 ... K R—Q 1; (threatening ... Q—Q 8 *ch*) and after 5 B—R 6, P—Kt 3; White, who has achieved his first object, has not yet obtained a satisfactory position, for his Kt is still badly placed and the Q R is not yet in play. Now new ideas must be evolved and a new series of moves is essential in order to overcome these various difficulties. It is impossible to foresee all the future moves in a game of chess; be satisfied if you can conceive a more or less extended series of moves which represent a logical plan; it will be a great step forward from the disconnected manner of the average amateur's play, which consists of separate moves, mostly lacking all sequence and logical connection.

To return to the position under examination, after 5 ... P—Kt 3; the white Knight would be well placed at its Q 4 or Q B 5, for which reason White plays 6 B—K 3. Black seeks to thwart the adversary's plans with 6 ... Q—Q 4; with a direct attack on the King. But now, with 7 Kt—R 5, White attacks the Q B. Thus White exchanges a weak Knight for a strong Bishop and eliminates, at the same time, the menace of the "two Bishops." Relying on his advantage in time, Black now plays 7 ... Q R—B 1; 8 Kt × B, Q × Kt.

The position (Diag. 15) is now simplified, but White

DIAGRAM 15

still has to cope with some difficulties; his Q R is still undeveloped, his K P is weak, his K R is more or less out of play for the moment; but there are fewer pieces and he can hope to equalise the game, though not without difficulty.

Let us recapitulate: we have seen that the complete analysis of a position followed by a synthesis of it as a whole, reveals to us its character and enables us to find the main idea underlying it. Accordingly our plan takes shape; we realise not only in which direction we must act, and at which objects we must aim, but also at what speed these objects have to be achieved.

The main thing is to see clearly the essence of the position, so as not to waste time and effort in attaining unimportant objects, and it is prudent to allow first for the opponent's moves so that our own ideas may be clear in our mind, allowing us to execute them at our leisure and not under pressure. Having a very precise notion of what we wish to do, we must ask ourselves how the opponent could interfere or prevent the execution of our plan.

Very often the real difficulty lies in the fact that the opponent, seeing our moves, can foresee our intentions and find an adequate reply in good time. The question therefore is how to conceal our intentions and how to lead our opponent astray with regard to them. It is true enough that, after the initial moves, we are not always sure that our opponent will fathom their trend; but we must always allow for this eventuality. To keep our intentions concealed is a problem in chess—luckily there are ways and means of solving it.

In the position shown in Diag. 16 the following moves were played: 1 ... B—R 6; 2 B—B 3, B—Kt 5; 3 B—Kt 2, B—R 6; 4 B—B 3, B—Kt 5; and only

DIAGRAM 16

White: Réti; *Black:* Alekhine
Baden-Baden, 1925

after White retired the B to R 1, did Black by 5 ...
P—K R 4; initiate an attack which secured him the
victory. Why this repetition of moves? Here is the
answer. For the attack in question, aimed at White's
K Kt 3, it was inopportune to have a white Bishop at
his K Kt 2 or K B 3. Only after White had given up
occupying these squares did Black proceed with his
intended attack. There is no doubt that this repetition
of moves deceived White, who, seeing his adversary's
indecision and his apparent willingness to accept a draw,
was induced to overestimate his own prospects and to
play for a win.

Another, and perhaps more striking, example is shown
in Diag. 17. Here the continuation was as follows:
1 R—Q 3, R—Kt 7; 2 B—Kt 1, Q—R 8; 3 B—B 2,
R—Kt 8. We see that White has made three perfectly
useless moves, without any significance, which not only
allowed the adverse Q and R to penetrate into his

DIAGRAM 17

White: Lasker; *Black:* Showalter
Cambridge Springs, 1904

position, but even induced them to do so. But it was in fact only a *ruse de guerre*, for with the departure from its camp of Black's heavy artillery, White was able to initiate a decisive attack, forcing the enemy's surrender in a few moves: 4 Kt—B 6, R—R 8; 5 Q—Kt 7, Kt—Kt 2; 6 Q—K B 7, R—Kt 8 *ch*; 7 K—B 3.

In both cases the means employed were rather crude; they succeeded thanks to the opponent's mistakes. But there are more subtle manœuvres which leave the adversary in doubt as to our intentions—threats neither direct nor too immediate. It would be idle to pretend that such methods are always at our disposal, but it is of some value, in choosing between several continuations, to take into account which of them is the least obvious and therefore the harder to parry.

4. TACTICAL POSSIBILITIES

In the preceding chapters we have spoken mainly of

general ideas and strategic plans. But in almost every game tactical possibilities in great numbers are likely, and it is important to learn how to take advantage of such opportunities. An astute player, thanks to his tactical ability, will succeed in saving many a lost game. It is quite easy to become the slave to a preconceived idea, and, whilst following it up methodically, to overlook a clandestine mate, subtly engineered by the opponent. A pedant, a blind worshipper of logic, is at times caught napping by an apparently fantastic scheme. Patiently pursuing a dim and distant object, a player often succumbs to a trap, especially if he has failed to take timely precautions and has unconcernedly and strictly adhered to his selected line of play. And how many opportunities are overlooked and left unexploited !

An opponent's oversight, a mistake, a weak move—such opportunities must be seized on the instant; a move later, and the chance will have gone. At times there arises a question of principle: shall we forgo our strategic plan in favour of a tactical diversion, which may be more lucrative ? Although such opportunities, both in attack and defence, must be utilised whenever possible, the strategic plan can still remain the basis of our play. But sad would be the fate of the strategist who, having formulated his plan, thought that he could go to sleep, nothing more being required of him.

Tactical opportunities may lead to simple manœuvres; but they are the mainspring of many of the most sparkling combinations. Tactics therefore require special attention in any book dealing with the subject of combinations.* It will be sufficient in the present volume to give a few illustrations.

Cf. my book "The Art of Chess Combination" (Chatto & Windus).

In Diag. 18 White is conducting a vigorous K side attack, the position of Black's King being seriously compromised.

DIAGRAM 18

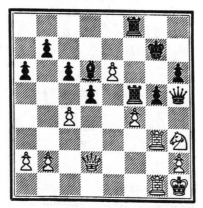

White: Alekhine; *Black:* Tylor
Margate, 1937

The game continued as follows:

1 Kt × P, B × P (capturing the Knight spells the loss of the Queen); 2 Q—B 3 *ch*, R (B 1)—B 3; 3 Kt—K 4 *dis. ch*, B × R; 4 R × B *ch*, K—R 1; 5 Q × R *ch*, R × Q; 6 R—Kt 8 *ch*, K × R; 7 Kt × R *ch*, followed by 8 Kt × Q. We have here a magnificent example of the "Kt combination," the basis of which is the unguarded position of Black's Queen at her K R 4. The strategic conception remains the same: attack against the King's field by means of the opening of the K Kt file; but this unfortunate position of the black Queen affords the tactical opportunity of a sudden and beautiful conclusion.

Observe that such tactical turns do not of necessity divert the player from his original strategic plan, and that at times, as in this instance, they further its execution.

Their conception, however, is frequently much more complicated. The position in Diag. 19 is such an example on the same theme.

DIAGRAM 19

White: Andreiev; *Black:* Dolookhanow
Leningrad, 1935

At first sight, no Kt combination appears to be possible here for no basis can be discerned on which it could be built up.

It is easy to see that Black must attack the King's position, but his opponent can do likewise and, it seems, with better chances, as the position of Black's King is open and White's B—Kt 1, carries a disagreeable threat. There are, however, two weaknesses in White's camp. The King is none too well placed and the Queen at K 3 is unguarded. The following combination is comparatively easy to find: 1 ... Q × P; 2 P × Q, B × P *ch*; 3 K—Kt 1, Kt—B 6 *ch*; 4 K—R1, and the King is in a perfect stalemate position. The problem is how to take advantage of the fact. An unimaginative player would never have found the cunning 4 ... B—Kt 7 *ch*;

5 K × B, Kt × R *ch*; attacking the Queen. Here, then, is the combination for which we were looking ! The only flaw is that the Rook is guarded by its companion.; as soon as this fact becomes clear, the whole combination becomes practicable. The initial move must be 1 ... K R × B; and, after 2 R × R, the combination shown above can be effected.

Anyone seeing this combination for the first time, with its initial sacrifice of the exchange seemingly entirely disconnected from the proceedings on the other wing, might well think it a miracle and the work of a genius. The retro-analysis to which we have subjected the position shows us the inner workings of the combination and, although no one would deny the talent of the player who conceived it, there is no doubt that logical reasoning and a little imagination should suffice for its creation.

A far more difficult problem occurs when a tactical possibility implies a complete reversal of strategic policy, and more so when the general plan is abandoned in favour of a combination without forced material gain.

Many games have been drawn, or even lost, through an opponent, faced with a winning attack, tendering an unobtrusive little pawn as a conciliatory bait: the attacker is content with this "bird-in-the-hand" and gives up his attack or his strategic plan, which might have overwhelmed his opponent, only to find that his small gain in material is insufficient to ensure victory or, worse still, that the initiative passes to the other side and he loses a game which he ought to have won. And yet the case in which there is a gain in material is the easiest of all to assess, for there should be little difficulty in calculating whether this gain is greater or smaller than the advantage that could be expected from the normal execution of the original plan. As Alekhine asserts, a gain in mrialate should only be a means of improving a positional advantage. But if a positional advantage should result in either case ? How can the difference be assessed ? Supposing we are carrying out subtle manœuvres on a flank with the object of paralysing the enemy forces, and now we find an easy tactical way of securing an advantage in another quarter, should we renounce our strategic intentions ? Has our opponent overlooked it or is it a trap ? Our forces are ideally placed for the execution of our original plan; will they be as active in the new circumstances ? Will the unexpected gain be sufficient to win ? The whole of our preliminary and imaginative work becomes futile: will our will to win, our creative power, prevail under the new conditions ? There are so many difficult questions of a technical, a sporting and a psychological nature to answer.

In Diag. 20 White exercises a vigorous pressure in the centre with attacking threats against the King. Should Black not exchange pawns at his K B 5, White

DIAGRAM 20

White: Kostitsch; *Black:* Znosko-Borovsky
Nice, 1930

will continue with P—B 5, and P—K Kt 4, and a
storming advance of all the pawns. But after the exchange White threatens to advance his K P, and after
... P×K P; P—Q 6, threatens to win the Q B; the
increased power of the Q P in itself justifies the advance.
Against this danger, after White's first move 1 Q—B 3,
Black played as follows: 1 ... P×P; 2 P×P, and now
tendered the first bait by 2 ... P—Q Kt 4. Thus White
is set the first problem: should he accept this tactical
sacrifice and relax his pressure in the centre?—e.g.,
3 P×P, P×P; 4 Kt×P, Q—Kt 3; 5 Kt—B 3, P—B 5
dis. ch; and Black recovers his pawn or obtains an active
and promising share in the play. White therefore rightly
ignored this tactical diversion. He played: 3 P—K 5,
and Black offered a second bait by playing 3 ... P—Kt 5;
again White can win a pawn by 4 P×Kt, P×Kt;
5 P×P, P×B; (... K B×P; 6 B×P) 6 P×B (Q) *ch*,
K × Q; 7 R—Kt 1. Relying on his positional superiority and the soundness of his strategy, White also
ignored this fresh attempt, but he made the mistake of
aiming at the gain of a Bishop instead of sustaining the
existing pressure; instead of playing 4 Kt—K 4, Kt × Kt;
5 Q × Kt, P—Kt 3; 6 Kt—Q 3, B—Kt 2; 7 Q R—K 1,
he played 4 Kt—R 4, forcing Black to follow his lead,
but getting a piece out of play. Now 4 ... P×P;
5 P—Q 6, Q × P; 6 Q × B, P—K 5; and White's Queen
is shut out, which affords Black a decisive advantage.

After having resisted on two occasions the tactical
temptation of a gain in material, White was wrong in
yielding the third time; the capture of the Bishop was
made at the cost of the essence of his plan to overwhelm
the enemy in the centre. On that account this example
is most instructive.

PART II. THE MIDDLE GAME

I. THE STAGES OF THE MIDDLE GAME

THE middle game forms a complete whole, distinct from the opening and the end game which are subject to laws of their own.

In spite of this fundamental unity, the middle game itself is divided into three well defined parts. These are the middle game proper, and the transition from the opening into the middle game and from the middle game into the end game. In the first of these transitory passages the tribulations of the preceding phase still weigh heavily, and in the last the cares and tribulations of the forthcoming end game must be taken into account. Common sense tells us that these intermediate manœuvres must be studied before we concentrate on the complete analysis of the middle game.

1. BETWEEN THE OPENING AND THE MIDDLE GAME

(a) *Special Characteristics*

Theoretically, the opening is completed when all the pieces are developed and ready for concerted action. In practice it ends where "the book" leaves off. Thus it often happens that, on leaving the beaten track, we must still think of completing our development, whilst some of the pieces are already engaged in battle. This state of things sets any player a problem requiring delicate and elastic treatment. To add to the difficulties, it is a fact that at this precise stage of the opening the position is not yet clarified, and it is difficult to settle on any definite plan of action. Even the most experienced masters have, at this stage, their moments of hesitation, of groping; they then make waiting or developing moves, improve their position without incurring any commitments. For a less mature amateur it is even more difficult. No wonder that this is the phase in which, not quite knowing what to do, the average player makes small mistakes which cost him the game. His game gradually deteriorates and the initiative passes to his opponent.

If we had to deal only with even positions of no pronounced character, we could study them as and when they occur and there would be no call for a separate analysis. But what adds to the difficulty of such positions is the fact that any move we make might lead us against our will into strategic conceptions of which we do not know the value; not only that, but every move by our opponent sets us not only tactical problems, which we must try to solve to our advantage, but strategic ones also. Whilst in the middle game an isolated move can hardly alter a sound strategic idea, in the phase at present under consideration, every move can initiate a different strategic conception, and if we do not realise this at the moment, we unsuspectingly pursue the chosen path, which now has become a *cul-de-sac* leading nowhere.

It is easy thus to realise how difficult is the task which awaits us at this stage, and it is not surprising that players are not always equal to it. We may add that the loss of a *tempo* in the opening can seldom be made good, so that waiting moves or even mechanical developing moves can lead to the loss of a game.

We must be doubly careful at this stage of the game, which undoubtedly is one of extreme difficulty. It is more difficult than the opening which is known through

the analysis of the theorists, or the middle game in which
we can at least find our way, thanks to the object, more
or less clear, which we have in view.

(b) Examples of various Openings and their transition into the Middle Game

Let us examine the position in Diag. 21, which is
known to all chess players and particularly to those who

DIAGRAM 21

practise the Queen's Gambit. The usual move for
Black is here 7 ... P—B 3; after which the possible
continuations are sufficiently well known.

Let us suppose that Black plays a different move
and we shall see with what problems White is
immediately faced. First we shall examine 7 ... P—
Q Kt 3.

This move discloses Black's intention of developing a
Bishop at Q Kt 2: therefore our first and immediate
reply is 8 P × P, P × P; closing the diagonal for a long
time to come if not permanently. Another characteristic of the move in question stands revealed : the

apparent weakness of the white squares on Black's
Queen's side. The question then arises: how can White
take advantage of this state of things ? If he does not
Black will post his B at Q Kt 2 and play ... P—Q B 4;
the secondary object of ... P—Q Kt 3. Perhaps a concerted action by our Q and K B may provide the solution;
therefore: 9 Q—R 4, P—B 4; 10 B—Kt 5, B—Kt 2;
11 B—B 6, B × B; 12 Q × B, R—B 1; 13 Q—R 4,
Kt—K 5; and White has nothing, his K B, which alone
could have exploited the weakness of the white squares,
having disappeared.

Let us make another attempt: 9 B—Kt 5, B—Kt 2;
10 Q—R 4, P—Q R 3; 11 B × Q Kt, Kt × B; 12
B × B, Q × B; 13 Q—Kt 3, Q—Q 3; 14 Castles, Q R—
K 1; and again Black has achieved equality.

Apparently Black's 7 ... P—Q Kt 3; gives White no
opportunity of obtaining an immediate advantage. White
must therefore continue his development, without, however, losing sight of the fact that after ... P—Q B 4;
Black will have a majority of pawns on the Q side.
White must seek counter-opportunities elsewhere, and a
K side attack is indicated. Therefore we play: 9 B—Q 3,
B—Kt 2; 10 Castles, P—B 4; 11 Kt—K 5, P—Q R 3;
12 P—B 4, P—B 5; 13 B—Kt 1, P—Kt 4; 14 P—B 3,
etc. And now the lines of play on either side have
become clear. It can even be said that White's strategic
plan was thrust upon him by Black's manœuvres on the
Q side. His moves Kt—K 5, and P—B 4, become the
logical sequel not only to his own 9th move but to the
preceding move by Black. And thus we see that a
simple pawn-move may lead to a sudden change in
strategic planning if only sufficient attention is given to it.

Let us now suppose that Black, instead of 7 ... P—

Q Kt 3; plays 7 ... P—Q R 3; a move, it would seem, without importance — another simple pawn - advance devoid of direct threats, and yet . . . what an immediate change in the situation ! We perceive without much difficulty what Black intends to do: ... P × P; followed by ... P—Kt 4; and ... P—B 4; mobilising the Queen's side.

We can avoid this danger by playing P × P, but we must first ascertain whether we can derive some tactical advantage from this move. If we play, for instance, 8 P—B 5, Black must reply with 8 ... P—B 3; and a certain weakness at his Q Kt 3 makes itself felt. But can we benefit from it ? Let us try: 9 B—Q 3, P—Q Kt 3; 10 P—Q Kt 4, P—Q R 4; 11 P—Q R 3, R P × P; 12 R P × P, P × P; 13 Kt P × P, Castles; 14 Castles, Q—R 4; after which Black has the initiative on the Q side, and our advanced Q B P is of little value.

We must therefore give up this tactical scheme, which promises no real advantage, and revert to our strategic idea: 8 P × P, P × P; 9 B—Q 3, P—B 4 (if instead Black plays 9 ... P—B 3; his 7 ... P—Q R 3; proves to be worse than useless); 10 P × P, Kt × P; 11 Castles, Kt—K 3; 12 B—R 4, and White maintains the initiative without affording Black the counter-chances which he obtained in the preceding variation.

We observe how ideas can change in the advanced stage of the opening and how logical reasoning can show us the proper course to follow.

We shall now show our readers a few examples of this advanced stage in various openings, without lengthy commentaries. They will illustrate the correct handling of this intermediate phase of the game.

Diag. 22 represents a familiar position in the "Dragon" variation of the Sicilian Defence.

DIAGRAM 22

White: Heilmann; *Black:* Vidmar
Barmen, 1905

After 1 B—B 3, R—B 1; 2 Kt—Kt 3, B—K 3; 3 Kt—Q 5, Kt—Q 2; 4 P—B 3, R—K 1; 5 P—Q R 4, we reach the position in Diag. 23, in which a definite

DIAGRAM 23

plan is taking shape and in which White has obtained a

real advantage in that Black's Queen's wing is in jeopardy, whilst the weakness of White's Q Kt P and the danger threatened by Black's open Q B file have both been eliminated by the advance of the Q B P.

Without entering into a discussion of the relative merits of the play of the two opponents, let us say, in passing, that White's advantage is due to Black's faulty second move. Had he played 2 ... Kt—Q R 4; (instead of 2 ... B—K 3;) 3 Kt × Kt, Q × Kt; 4 K R—Q 1, P—Kt 5; (Löwenfisch-Cohn, Carlsbad, 1911) he would have avoided the danger. But 2 ... Q—B 2; would not have helped, e.g.: 3 Kt—Q 5, Kt × Kt; 4 P × Kt, Kt— Q 1; 5 P—B 3, Kt—Kt 2; 6 K R—K 1, with advantage to White (Marco-Weiss, Match, Vienna, 1895). More than in any other part of the game, a single inexact move at this stage is liable to alter the whole aspect of a position.

In the next example (Diag. 24) from a Dutch Defence, White is uncertain as to which course to pursue and

DIAGRAM 24

White: Capablanca; *Black:* Alekhine
Nottingham, 1936

allows Black time and opportunity of completing his development and seizing the initiative.

The play went as follows: 1 ... B—B 3; 2 Kt—Q Kt 5, Q—K 2; 3 B—K 3, P—Q·R 3; 4 Kt—Q 4, B—Q 2; 5 Q R—B 1, Q R—K 1; 6 P—Q Kt 4, P—Q Kt 3; (see Diag. 25) and now the respective plans of both

DIAGRAM 25

players have become apparent: White wishes to "work" on the Q side, where Black has a majority of pawns, and to break up the pawn formation, whilst Black is aiming at the King's side and the centre. A strange move by White 7 Kt—B 3, losing yet another *tempo*, turns out well for him, as Black is tempted to indulge in a tactical combination: 7 ... Kt—B 6; 8 R—Q 3, P—B 5 ?; 9 P × P, B—B 4; in order to win the exchange. The result is a bad game for Black: another instance in which a tactical diversion proves abortive and the renunciation of the strategic plan leads to the loss of the game.

Diag. 26 shows a position resulting from the Cambridge Springs variation of the Queen's Gambit. After the initial moves: 1 P—Q 4, P—Q 4; 2 P—Q B 4, P—K 3;

DIAGRAM 26

White: Capablanca; *Black:* Alekhine
Match, 1927

3 Kt—Q B 3, Kt—K B 3; 4 B—Kt 5, Q Kt—Q 2;
5 P—K 3, P—B 3; 6 Kt—B 3, Q—R 4; 7 Kt—Q 2,
B—Kt 5; 8 Q—B 2, P × P; 9 B × Kt, Kt × B; 10
Kt × P, Q—B 2; 11 P—Q R 3, B—K 2; White gradually initiates a struggle round Black's Queen's side
pawns, first of all preventing him from freeing his game
by ... P—B 4. Black, wishing to ease the pressure, plays

DIAGRAM 27

the unconsidered move 15 ... P—Q R 4; after which his pawns at Q Kt 3 and Q B 3 become very weak and one of them is irretrievably lost. Here is the continuation, which leads to the position in Diag. 27: 12 P—K Kt 3, B—Q 2; 13 B—Kt 2, Castles K R; 14 P—Q Kt 4, P—Q Kt 3; 15 Castles K R, P—Q R 4; 16 Kt—K 5, P × P; 17 P × P, R × R; 18 R × R, R—B 1; 19 Kt × B, Q × Kt; 20 Kt—R 4, Q—Q 1; 21 Q—Kt 3, Kt—Q 4; 22 P—Kt 5, P × P; 23 Q × K P, etc.

Here is another example of an Indian Defence. After 1 P—Q 4, Kt—K B 3; 2 P—Q B 4, P—K 3; 3 Kt—K B 3, P—Q Kt 3; 4 P—K Kt 3, B—Kt 2; 5 B—Kt 2, B—Kt 5 ch; 6 B—Q 2, B × B ch; 7 Q × B, P—Q 3; 8 P—Q 5, P—K 4; we reach the position shown in Diag. 28, which is of frequent occurrence in this opening.

DIAGRAM 28

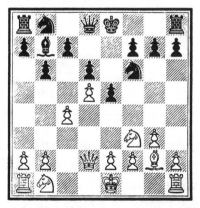

The advance of Black's K P clearly indicates the line of play which White will follow: advance of the K B P to its 4th, and the occupation of K B 5 by his K Kt. To prevent this, Black will have to play ... P—Kt 3; giving White another objective, since Black will seek to

place his Q Kt at Q B 4, from which square White
will dislodge it by P—Q Kt 4. Here are the moves
played in a recent game: 9 Kt—B 3, Q Kt—Q 2; 10
Castles K R, Castles; 11 Kt—K 1, Q—K 2; 12 P—K 4,
P—Kt 3; 13 Kt—B 2, P—Q R 4; 14 Kt—K 3,
Kt—B 4; 15 Q—B 2, B—B 1; 16 P—Kt 3, B—Q 2;
17 P—Q R 3, Kt—R 4; 18 P—Q Kt 4, Kt—Q Kt 2;
19 Q R—K 1, Kt—Kt 2; 20 Q—Q 2, Kt—Q 1;
21 P—B 4, P.—K B 3; etc. (Diag. 29). We see that

DIAGRAM 29

White: Euwe; *Black:* Flohr
Match, 1932

White has initiated an energetic attack, against which
Black has prepared a stubborn defence, which is reminis-
cent of a variation of the Ruy Lopez with two pawns at
K B 3 and K Kt 3 and two Knights at K B 2 and K Kt 2.

Considerations of space prevent us from giving more
numerous examples. But all the positions which we
have examined teach the same principle, namely: that
here, to an even greater degree than in the middle game
proper, the strategic idea is of far greater importance

than tactical eventualities or the development of backward pieces.   At the same time we are not yet committed
to any particular plan: we can make our choice, we can
even change our original idea.   This is an advantage as
it confers a certain freedom on our play, but a disadvantage, in that committing ourselves to a faulty plan would
threaten to ruin the whole of our game.

2.   BETWEEN MIDDLE GAME AND END GAME

(a) Special Characteristics

Entirely different worries beset the player when the
end game is in sight.   To be sure, if we have obtained
a substantial advantage in material, for instance a piece,
we can embark on the end game with entire confidence,
if not with a feeling of certainty.   But   the advantage
gained is not great, say only a pawn, or some advantage
in position, the whole outlook is different.   We may
notice, often too late, that what appeared in the middle
game to be an undoubted "pull," has become in the end
game a weakness, and features in the enemy's position
to which we gave no thought have become a first class
weapon in his hands.   Imagine that you have been conducting a violent attack on the K side and that your
opponent has an isolated but passed Q R P.   In the
circumstances you did not give it a thought and rather
looked on it as a weakness.   Now your attack fails to
lead to a mate or to bring you any other advantage, and
you see the despised pawn make its way unhindered to
the queening square !
What is to be done in such cases ?   What is the
remedy ?   Certainly not an exaggerated caution, which

leads you to think at all times, from the very opening, about a possible end game. It would be unthinkable; no attack would succeed, for, in order to conduct a middle game successfully, all our forces must participate without restrictions and to the bitter end.

But a counsel of wisdom is this: as soon as the play shows signs of leading into an end game, reconsider the position from that point of view. If you feel uneasy about it, defer the end game as long as you can and utilise the time gained in improving your chances for the ending. If, on the contrary, your chances are good, bring about the end game as quickly as you can.

If you are on the defensive in a difficult position, this transition from the middle to the end game may spell salvation if you know how to build up your defence to that end. If you have the initiative, however, and your advantage in the middle game is small, which means that your direct attack is little likely to win through, then the utmost caution is required. Avoid all weaknesses which may weigh in the balance in the end game, and the sooner you start preparations for the ending, the better.

It is sound strategy to bring about an end game as soon as an advantage in the middle game proves insufficient to win by direct attack; this advantage, however, must be kept up into the next phase where it can lead to success.

(b) Examples of various Endings and how they arise from the Middle Game

It is impossible here to review the various elements of favourable end game positions as opposed to those of middle game. We must take for granted that they are familiar to our readers. It will suffice to give a few examples to illustrate the different aspects of these two phases of the game.

DIAGRAM 30

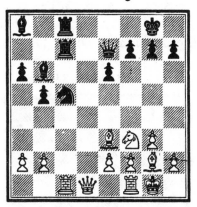

White: Capablanca; *Black:* Reshevsky
Nottingham, 1936

In Diag. 30 Black's development is clearly superior. He has 14 moves to his credit as against 7 by White. At the same time there is no weakness in White's camp and his chances for the end game are perhaps slightly better owing to the advance of Black's Q side pawns. White therefore brought about a succession of exchanges, trying to create some weaknesses in the black position. Black, on the other hand, realising that he would have little chance in an end game, tried in vain to prepare an attack. In so doing he actually created a weakness in his own camp—an isolated Q P on a white square with a white Bishop, leaving White with a Knight on a strong supporting black square, which should be a sufficient advantage for an end game.

The play went as follows: 1 P—Kt 3, Kt—Q 2;

2 R × R, R × R; 3 B × B, Kt × B; 4 Q—Q 4, Kt—
Q 4; 5 R—Q 1, P—B 3; 6 Kt—K 1, B—Kt 2;
7 B × Kt, P × B; 8 P—K 3, Q—K 5; 9 P—K R 4,
P—Q R 4; 10 P—B 3, Q × Q; 11 R × Q, R—B 8;
12 K—B 2, R—R 8; 13 R—Q 2, P—R 5; 14 Kt—Q 3,
R—Q Kt 8; 15 R—Kt 2, R × R *ch*; 16 Kt × R, which
brings us to the position in Diag. 31. Black has a lost

DIAGRAM 31

game owing to the weakness of his Bishop and of his
Q Kt P and Q P. It is clear that he should at all cost
have avoided exchanges, especially of his Q and his
second Rook.

It is most difficult correctly to assess the value of
minor pieces in an end game; which one of two Bishops
is it best to preserve; which is the stronger, a Knight or
a Bishop ? etc. In most cases the player may know the
answer perfectly well and yet remain with the "wrong"
piece, because he had it before the end game was even
considered.

In the position shown in Diag. 32, which was given
up as a draw, the black Knight is clearly superior to

DIAGRAM 32

White: Botvinnik; *Black:* Winter
Nottingham, 1936

White's Bishop, and had not this game been played in the last round of the tournament, it is more than likely that Black would have scored a win by bringing his King up to the Q side and posting his Knight at Q B 5. The position is particularly interesting because White's Bishop looks very strong. All the black pawns are on white squares and White's centre pawns on black squares, the best possible arrangement for White. Yet the Bishop has no scope at all and is reduced to the defensive. The same applies to the white Rook. On the other hand, the black pieces have complete freedom of action ; they have more space, are aggressive, and the King can easily co-operate in the struggle.

What has been said of the pieces applies in an equal measure to the pawns; we have seen how important a part they play in a game of chess. Very often, however, their function in the end game is totally different.

Examine the position in Diag. 33. White has a marked advantage and attacking chances. He did not make the best of the position and failed to exploit his advantage or to turn it into a decisive one. Finally he made the mistake of playing a pawn to K B 6. At first sight this pawn may seem to threaten many dangers, including several threats of mate.

DIAGRAM 33

White: Capablanca; *Black:* Alekhine
Match, 1927

By skilful play Black brought about many exchanges, leading into the end game, with the result that White remained with a doubled pawn requiring constant attention. Only with the utmost difficulty could White have obtained a draw against Black's strong passed pawn. As it was, the task required such precision that the problem proved too much for White, who lost a game which in its middle phase looked like a probable win for him.

The following are the moves from the position in Diag. 33: 1 Kt—K 5, P—Kt 3; 2 Kt—Kt 4, B—Kt 2; 3 P—K 5, P—K R 4; 4 Kt—K 3, P—Q B 4; 5 Kt P × P, P × P; 6 P—Q 5, P × P; 7 Kt × P, Q—K 3; 8 Kt—

B 6 *ch*, B × Kt; 9 P × B, R × R *ch*; 10 R × R, B—B 3;
and the position in Diag. 34 is reached.

DIAGRAM 34

We shall, in the course of our studies, have occasion
to examine positions in which one or the other player
deliberately brings about an end game either in order to
increase his advantage or conversely to minimise the
drawbacks of his position. It is well to repeat here that,
even before such a decision is under consideration, there
comes a time when the position must be reviewed from
the point of view of end game possibilities. If we put
this advice into practice we shall undoubtedly save a
good number of games which would otherwise be lost.
There is no doubt that frequently we are faced with
defeat through carelessly omitting this eventuality from
our calculations.

II. SUPERIORITY IN POSITION

1. Superiority in the various Elements

Everyone knows what superiority in position means and that such superiority can exist even when there is a distinct inferiority in some elements. It is desirable to have the advantage in all three elements, but it happens far more frequently that an advantage in one element is accompanied by a disadvantage in another. As we have seen, it can even happen that an advantage in all three elements fails to insure positional superiority. In order to recall this fact to the reader's mind we give an additional example in Diag. 35.

DIAGRAM 35

White: Miss Menchik; *Black:* Znosko-Borovsky
London, 1937

Here White has the advantage in material—two pawns; in time—15 moves against 10; in space—P's at K 5 and K B 6. But in spite of mating threats White's game is lost. Black plays: 1 ... R × Kt*ch*; 2 P × R,

Q—B 3; and there is no defence against the threatened mate. 3 B—B 3, B × R *ch*; etc.

Such cases, however, are exceptional and an advantage in all elements normally represents a real superiority in position. However, an external analysis is not sufficient to reveal to us the inner significance of a position and its character.

It would be unwise to put too much trust in advantages in one or more elements and to concentrate on their increase. What is of real moment to us is the advantage in the position as a whole. This, however, can be ascertained only by an analysis of all the elements. In addition, it is not sufficient to realise that the position is superior; it is essential to find the exact degree of superiority and in what it consists. If the advantage be but slight, it is necessary to proceed slowly, without forcing matters or taking risks. If, however, the advantage be overwhelming, there is justification (one might almost say it was a duty) for initiating a vigorous attack, for an advantage which is not exploited is frittered away and more likely than not passes to the adversary. That is a moral obligation in chess if we are to believe Steinitz and Lasker.

Finally, one should realise with the utmost clearness in which particular element superiority exists, as the manner of its treatment varies in each of the three elements; an advantage in space cannot be increased in the same manner as an advantage in time.

A study of positions in which advantages in various elements exist will serve as an introduction to an analysis of the line of thought to be followed in superior positions and of the means available for exploiting such superiority. This will allow us to reduce our remarks to a minimum

and merely to quote the moves played with a few variations. We shall thus be able to give more numerous
examples.

One could ignore positions in which there is an
advantage in material, for there seems little to be said
about a position in which one player has an extra piece
or pawn. Yet such positions frequently present a
common characteristic.

A player, having gained an advantage in material, is
apt to assume the defensive, playing a passive game or
trying to bring about an end game. Very often these
tactics lead to disaster or, at best, to a draw. The
opponent takes the initiative and succeeds in obtaining
a positional advantage which makes up for the material
he has lost. It would be equally futile for the stronger
side to embark on risky and hazardous undertakings:
"Only the weak trust to chance." But there is no doubt
that an advantage in material, be it only that of a pawn,
justifies far more audacious measures, both in attack and
defence, than would be permissible in a perfectly even
position.

The difficulty in these cases resides precisely in the
fact that very often a more or less marked positional
advantage sets off the lack of material. We may have to
exploit an extra pawn in spite of an adverse positional
advantage.

In the position shown in Diag. 36 Black has an extra
pawn, his only advantage, for he has two pieces out of
play on the Q side, whilst on the K side White is conducting a dangerous attack. In addition White is a
tempo ahead. Suppose for a moment that Black were
without a Q R P; with equal forces White would have
all the advantage. With a passed pawn and the attack

DIAGRAM 36

White: Marshall; *Black:* Capablanca
Match, 1909

he could at once aim at forcing a win. As it is he has
to proceed slowly and methodically, as is demanded by
the small advantage he possesses, for he would be lost
as soon as the adversary's Q side pawns were able to
start their advance. Black's unobtrusive Q R P hampers
White's game and even affects his K side attack.

White therefore plays:

    1   Kt—R 5   P—Kt 3
    2   P—Q 6

Black cannot capture this pawn as he would lose his
Q R.

    2   ...   Q—K 3

Without his extra pawn Black's defence would be
wholly inadequate as White would then exchange Queens,
doubling and isolating pawns on the K file, as well as
threatening to win a pawn by Kt—B 6 *ch.* But as
matters stand, Black's extra pawn, though inactive at the
moment, becomes a real threat as soon as White ceases
to attack or permits exchanges to take place. This

shows that the player who has an advantage in material
can take a certain amount of risk and can allow his
position to be weakened in a manner which, without his
extra material, might easily prove fatal.

3   Q—Kt 5   K—R 1

The pawn is still immune from capture: 3 ... R × P;
4 R × R, Q × R; 5 Q—R 6, Q—B 1; 6 Kt—B 6 *ch*,
and 7 Q × P *mate*.

4   Kt—B 6   R × P
5   R × R   Q × R

And thus Black has won a second pawn and is still
able to cope with White's attack.

Another way of turning a material advantage to
account is to surrender it at the proper time in exchange
for a substantial advantage in position. This applies in
particular to the opening, where it is bad policy to strive
at all costs to maintain some material advantage. In
that phase of the game, positional considerations are
paramount: that is the idea underlying all gambits. We
must warn, however, against such a surrender being
made without proper thought, as a matter of routine.
In chess no effort should turn out to have been made
in vain, and no advantage must be surrendered before
it has been, as far as possible, turned to account.

In giving our attention to positions which show an
advantage in either time or space, we immediately notice
a great difference. Such an advantage is definitely positional, and unlike the advantage in material, it confers
special characteristics on the position.

Let us first examine the advantage in time. As
already stated, this is the hardest case to diagnose. It
is even more difficult to preserve. It is a curious characteristic of this element that it cannot be increased

indefinitely: there comes a time when our opponent will even up matters. It cannot even be maintained at a steady level, for every move which fails to increase the lead allows our opponent to make up leeway in his development, and thus to improve matters for himself as regards the element of time. In addition, an advantage in time is in itself insufficient to enforce a win. It must be transformed into an advantage in another ele ent. This is the most critical moment which often decides the fate of the game, and one where we always risk forfeiting our advantage.

The main thing in chess is, as we have stated before, the conflict of chess ideas. But, even so, it is always important to realise clearly the exigencies of the three elements, for on these our conduct of the game very frequently depends. If we fail to realise in which particular element we have an advantage, we may have the most brilliant ideas, but they must of necessity be aimless, and we shall be unable to select the proper method of carrying them out.

Let us examine Diag. 37.

This position illustrates our point particularly well: Black has only an advantage in time, whereas White has won a pawn and is far superior in space. Moreover, White has not a single weakness, and whatever Black may hope to achieve could only have this advantage in time as a basis.

As usual, the characteristics of the situation are ascertained after comparing the two positions. In this case the difference between the Bishops is important. White's Bishop is as yet undeveloped whilst the black Bishop occupies a long open diagonal, aiming at the Kt and at the Kt P behind it. If, on the other hand, the Kt moves,

DIAGRAM 37

White: Nimzowitsch; *Black:* Capablanca
St. Petersburg, 1914

the Q R P is in jeopardy. White will therefore require some considerable time to complete his development. Before the Kt is able to move it will be necessary to guard the Q R P, defend the Kt with the B, and move the Q R; then only will the Bishop obtain any freedom of action. Thus Black's advantage in time can become still more considerable.

But were Black content to watch his opponent's efforts to extricate his Q side without taking action, White would carry out his plan and, having at last mobilised his Bishop and, incidentally, made up for the time lost in winning a pawn, he would probably proceed to win the game on the strength of his extra pawn.

What is Black to do ? A further characteristic of the position now appears: the two open files on the Q side. On these files Black will be able to attack the pawns, and White's extra pawn will continue to require protection. If, however, Black simply brings up a Rook for the attack, he will lose still further time without making any real threat, and White's Queen will be able to return into camp. He must play a more subtle game, limiting White's freedom of action by constant attacks and varied threats. Hence his first move:

1   ...   K R—K 1

He attacks the K P, which immobilises White's Knight and compels White to make a defensive move.

2   Q—Q 3

White brings back his Q into his lines, but in so doing he relieves his pressure on Black's Q B P and restores to the black Queen her freedom of action. A move such as 2 P—K B 3, which will sooner or later have to be played, would be preferable. A player who is at a disadvantage in point of time should keep up any available threat.

2   ...   Q—K 3

A fresh threat.

3   P—B 3

Black's first attack is at an end. It is clear that it was only meant as a demonstration. What must he do now? The Rook's move liberated the Queen, the Queen moved to make room for the Knight. As the attack against the K P is at an end, the Knight, *via* Q 2, K 4, Q B 5, will attack the Q side and the Q Kt P, still further impeding the development of White's B. The black Knight retreats temporarily but opens the way for the Bishop, which also attacks the Q side.

3   ...   Kt—Q 2

White tries to parry the threat shown above by developing his pieces.

4   B—Q 2   Kt—K 4
5   Q—K 2   Kt—B 5

Now the Q Kt P is threatened. If 6 P—Q Kt 3, Kt × B; 7 Q × Kt, Q—K 4; etc.

       6   Q R—Kt 1   R—R 1

Again a threat. As can be easily seen, Black has managed to place his Rook on this file by means of continual threats, therefore without loss of time. All his pieces are now directed against the Q side, where the main action is being fought; by combining a threat with every move, he prevents his opponent from developing his pieces, whilst warding off these threats. So far he has succeeded admirably. Here, for instance, he threatens to win a pawn after 7 P—Q Kt 3, Kt × B.

       7   P—Q R 4   Kt × B

In order to bring the Queen into the game.

       8   Q × Kt   Q—B 5

Again P—Q Kt 3, is not feasible because of the threat to the Knight. Incidentally, Black threatens to win the Q R P by ... B × Kt; and if 9 Kt—K 2, the Q R P is lost. The best course in the circumstances would be 9 Kt—Q 1, giving up the extra pawn but relieving the adverse pressure.

       9   K R—Q 1   K R—Kt 1

Here Black could have won a pawn by ... B × Kt. The present threat, however, is to win two pawns by ... R × Kt P; R × R, B × Kt; Q—B 1, B × R; Q × B, Q × R P; but then White could reply with Q—Kt 7, threatening the backward Q B pawns.

The position is shown in Diag. 38. Summing up its main points, we see that Black has gained only one move, but that, on the other hand, he has gained much space. All his pieces occupy open lines and his Queen dominates the board. His advantage in time is now transferred to the element of space. It only remains for him to

DIAGRAM 38

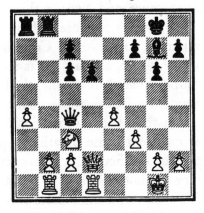

exchange it for a gain in material and the game is won for him.

	10	Q—K 3	R—Kt 5

Threatening B—Q 5.

	11	Q—Kt 5	B—Q 5 *ch*
	12	K—R 1	R (R 1)—Kt 1

Threatened with the loss of a piece, White is compelled to give up the exchange.

	13	R × B	Q × R

and the game is won for Black.

The most striking feature in this example is Black's admirable conduct of the game. The manner in which he exploited his advantage in time is beyond praise. Nearly every move contained a threat, which is the correct method of turning to account an advantage in time as opposed to an advantage in space, as we shall show later.

It is, of course, not essential that each threat should be direct and immediate: they may be distant threats, perhaps merely indicated by the moves as future contingencies. This is easy to understand. The player who

is in arrears in time has only to complete his development
to eliminate all pressure and two or three quiet moves
are often sufficient for this purpose. This the opponent
must seek, at all costs, to prevent. Constant threats are
the best means to this end, although it is clear that every
move must be subordinated to a general plan.

A difficult moment arises in these manœuvres when a
piece has to be transferred to another field, which necessarily gives the opponent some breathing space. In the
present example this difficulty is overcome with con-
summate mastery. Another piece is unmasked at the
critical time with a new and immediate threat.

Another delicate problem arises when the advantage
in time is to be transferred to another element. This
process is also carried out exceedingly well here; the act
of transformation is hardly noticeable.

The student would do well to study this game with
the greatest care: it is instructive in the highest degree.

All these processes will stand out even more clearly
when we compare them with those employed in positions
in which the advantage to be exploited is one of space.

Where an advantage in space exists, it means that the
opponent's movements are restricted; his pieces lack
space in which to radiate their full power. It is therefore
unnecessary to threaten the adversary; it is sufficient to
prevent his pieces from coming out from their narrow
space by controlling the squares in front of his position.
The advantage in space is less easily lost, and can increase
almost indefinitely. It is often permissible to lose time
so long as no pieces are actually withdrawn, and the
adverse forces are still further restricted by quiet
manœuvring. It is not necessary to transform this
advantage into a material one, and so this very critical

moment in the exploitation of advantages in time does not arise here. On the other hand, there is another and equally anxious time when the opponent, whose position is becoming more and more restricted, decides to give up some material in order to relieve the pressure. It then happens not infrequently that he is able to assume the initiative when our well-advanced forces are badly placed to resist this sudden and unexpected onslaught.

DIAGRAM 39

White: Lasker; *Black:* Capablanca
St. Petersburg, 1914

Diag. 39 will show this more clearly. Here time and force are equal on either side, but White has the advantage in space with two centre pawns on the fourth rank and two well-developed Knights. Black's forces occupy the first three ranks, with little hope of enlarging their scope. His greatest concern is the undeveloped state of his Q B. A useful post would be at Kt 2, from where, supported by the Rook, it would attack the K P. If this pawn advances, a splendid square at Black's K B 4 becomes available for his Kt.

As White has no threats at his disposal, except possibly P—B 5—B 6, which cannot be entertained for some time, he must proceed cautiously and continue a policy of restriction.

Black has an immediate threat, by ... B—Q B 4; pinning a Knight and occupying a fine diagonal. And now White plays: Kt—Kt 3. A strange move indeed, for not only is it devoid of threats but White has actually retreated one of his developed pieces ! An entirely different procedure from that shown in the preceding example (advantage in time). The explanation is that, with an advantage in space, it is less important to threaten the enemy than to prevent him from extricating himself from his cramped position and to deny him the possibility of making any threats himself. In the present instance the white Knight keeps the Bishop from his Q B 4 and also avoids being pinned.

1.   Kt—Kt 3   P—B 3

The object of this move is not only to prevent here and now the advance P—B 5—B 6, but principally to make the development of the Q B at Kt 2 possible and to open the long diagonal by ... P—Q B 4; which, at the moment, is not feasible because of the threat to the K B after P—K 5. In addition, White must reckon with the possibility of Black's Q B being developed at K 3 or even K Kt 5 now that a sanctuary is available for it at its B 2.

2 P—B 5

White forestalls this threat at once without himself threatening anything in particular unless it be the establishment, in the distant future, of a Kt at K 6. Incidentally, White creates a weakness for himself at K 5 for the sake of maintaining the pressure and of preserving his advantage in space.

2   ...   P—Q Kt 3

Black prepares the development of his B at Kt 2, now that K Kt 5 is no longer available. His position is one of great difficulty. If he keeps the Bishop on its diagonal Q B 1—K R 6 in order to guard his K 3, his position would remain restricted and White, after B—B 4, and Q R—Q 1, would have a splendid and untrammelled game, without any counter-chances for Black. On the other hand, after ... B—Kt 2 ; Black's K 3 remains defence-less and becomes a target for a virulent assault as the sequel shows.

3   B—B 4

To begin with, the K B is to be eliminated, and as the exchange is unavoidable, Black should have made it himself in order to gain a *tempo* and to avoid the creation of a weakness at his Q 3. He decides, however, to persevere in his development as planned and in the end he has to defend two weaknesses instead of one.

3   ...   B—Kt 2
4   B × B   P × B
5   Kt—Q 4

The first threat after four quiet moves. And what is the threat ? Simply to post his Kt at K 6. White's manœuvring has cost him a *tempo*, but in return he has increased his stranglehold. Black's only remaining chance lies in his attack on the K P and he cannot allow the white Kt to settle permanently on its K 6. Hence the necessity of advancing his Q B P and Q P.

He cannot prevent the Knight from moving to K 6, threatening Q 8; therefore he must move the Q R at once if it is to get into play at all.

5   ...   Q R—Q 1
6   Kt—K 6   R—Q 2

Observe that in achieving his aim White has made three "moves" less than his adversary. It is true that Black's gain in time—advance of the Q side pawns—is of no value. But it remains a fact: we have noted a similar occurrence in the preceding example, where an increase of the advantage in time was accompanied by a loss in space.

It is obvious that White will now attack the weak point at Black's Q 3.

　　　　　7　Q R—Q 1

How can the attack on the Q P be parried ? Either by guarding or by advancing it: this advance cannot take place at once as the pawn would be isolated and soon lost. Therefore ... P—B 4; would first be called for in order to keep his Q 4 under control of the Bishop. White must now guard his B P by P—K Kt 4, e.g.: 7 ... P—B 4; 8 P—K Kt 4, P—Q 4; 9 P × P, B × P; 10 Kt × B, R × Kt; 11 Kt—B 7, R × R; 12 R × R, R—Q B 1; 13 R—Q 7, and wins.

It follows that the Q P cannot advance and Black is reduced to a passive defence: such is the result of White's strategy.

7	...	Kt—B 1
8	R—B 2	P—Q Kt 4
9	K R—Q 2	Q R—K 2
10	P—Q Kt 4	

Anticipating the threat ... P—B 4.

10	...	K—B 2
11	P—Q R 3	

There is a basic difference between this game and the last. There are no threats from White, who merely continues to strengthen his position, restricting his opponent more and more and nullifying his attempts to free his game. Such tactics are possible only when there is an advantage in space and not in time.

Now at last we reach the critical moment mentioned above. Black has the opportunity of giving up the exchange for a pawn (11 ... R × Kt; 12 P × R *ch*, R × P;) and with the attack on the K P he would obtain unexpected chances.

To prove the soundness or otherwise of his sacrifice it would be necessary to play the game anew. But it can be stated that Black would remain with B, P and 3 moves for a Rook whilst White's advantage in space would have miraculously and suddenly disappeared. There is no doubt, however, that Black having let this chance pass by, has delivered himself into the hands of the enemy, who can now impose his will.

11	...	B—R 1
12	K—B 2	R—R 2
13	P—Kt 4	

The decisive assault now begins. White's advantage is overwhelming and the defence must break down somewhere.

13	...	P—R 3
14	R—Q 3	P—Q R 4

Useless as well as damaging. The opening of lines is of benefit only to the stronger party.

15	P—K R 4	P × P
16	P × P	R (R2)—K 2
17	K—B 3	R—Kt 1
18	K—B 4	P—Kt 3
19	R—Kt 3	P—Kt 4 *ch*
20	K—B 3	Kt—Kt 3
21	P × P	R P × P

The continuation is of no real interest for our purpose,

for Black, having lost his advantage in time, has nothing
to play for. White simply goes on demolishing his
opponent's position.

22	R—R 3	R—Q 2
23	K—Kt 3	K—K 1
24	Q R—K R 1	B—Kt 2
25	P—K 5	

At last the decisive break-through ! White eliminates
his weak pawn, the idea being to put the Knight in its
place, threatening the King and both Rooks.

25	...	Q P × P
26	Kt—K 4	Kt—Q 4
27	Kt (K 6)—B 5	B—B 1
28	Kt × R	B × Kt
29	R—R 7 and White won.	

This game admirably demonstrates how an advantage
in space should be increased without having recourse to
threats, which are the mainstay of operations where an
advantage in time is concerned.

This subject cannot be exhausted by two examples.
Others can be found in which the win is achieved in a
different manner. But the characteristic features of the
mode of treatment are illustrated sufficiently clearly in
these two cases for the amateur to master these difficulties
in his own play.

And now we can pass on to the next section dealing
with the evolving of an idea when exploiting a superior
position.

2. VARIOUS MEANS OF EXPLOITING AN ADVANTAGE

When a thorough analysis has revealed to us that we
possess a certain advantage, a good many questions

remain to be settled. It is not sufficient to know that we have the advantage, nor in what it consists, nor how big it is. Numerous problems demand to be solved and the same analysis usually provides the solution.

It certainly is a matter of satisfaction if the fate of the game can be decided by a brilliant combination, nor should one omit to make sure whether such an opportunity offers itself, or at least some tactical possibility. But such cases are of rare occurrence, and everyone knows that more often than not a long and arduous struggle is necessary in order to secure the victory. Did not Dr. Tarrasch say that the hardest task is to win a won game?

The lay-out of our own and of enemy pieces must be carefully examined and compared: this will usually indicate the character and venue of the action which is to be undertaken. We can thus ascertain whether we have immediate or future attacking chances, and whether or no an attack may lead to a mate. This is a question of the greatest importance, for if there is a probable mate no sacrifice is too great and every resource must be drawn upon to attain this object, even to neglecting all other parts of the board no matter at what hazard.

Where there is no chance of a mate—which can happen even in the case of a K side attack—caution is necessary; we may conduct an energetic attack, but if the result is but the gain of a pawn, we cannot afford to sacrifice, nor must we submit to a positional disadvantage on another part of the board.

Having established our opponent's chief weakness, which becomes our objective, we must settle the means of reaching it. Are the pieces alone sufficient? Will an assault by pawns be indispensable? Must we sacrifice

in order to open a file ? etc. There are very many cases
where our available forces are not suited for the attack
on a particular weakness. An adverse pawn on our
K R 7 may be weak, but we lack a white Bishop ! A
pawn at K Kt 7 is likely to fall, and we find that we
cannot post a Knight at K B 5 or K R 5.

We may not be able to solve all these problems as
soon as an attack seems to be both feasible and advantageous, but the solution will occur to us gradually in
the course of play. Therein lies the difference between
the strong player and the rank-and-file. The average
player fails even to consider all these questions, whilst
the expert attends to them early, at times even subconsciously.

Let us examine the position in Diag. 40. There are
numerous good moves and possible plans at White's
disposal.

DIAGRAM 40

White: Capablanca; *Black:* Janowski
St. Petersburg, 1914

White played 1 R—Kt 1, and Dr. Tarrasch remarked
in the book of the Tournament: "Reveals with brutal

frankness the plan of attack against which nothing can be done. The Q Kt P, supported by the Q R P, is to storm the hostile King's embattlements, impregnable though they may seem." 1 ... P—B 3; 2 P—Kt 4, Kt—B 2; 3 P—Q R 4, B × Kt; 4 R × B, P—Q Kt 3; 5 P—Kt 5, B P × P; 6 P × P, P—Q R 4; 7 Kt—Q 5, Q—B 4; 8 P—B 4, and the eminent annotator adds: "Again played with great precision. The attack is to be continued with Q—B 3, and P—Q 4." What has been achieved here with such apparent ease depends, in difficult positions, on a conception of the utmost accuracy. Side by side with a general plan of our play, we must have a plan of attack which is equally clear. The average player is content to make more or less plausible moves, advancing his pieces in the general direction of the objective, without troubling overmuch about the fundamentals of his attack. This is a pity; any efforts we make in obtaining a clear conception of the intended attack will reward us by the rapid and energetic development of the attack itself.

Similar questions are raised in the case of positional manœuvres, though here the same degree of precision is neither necessary nor attainable. For here the moves of neither player are compulsory; there are no direct threats, and there often is no clearly-defined objective.

But nevertheless we must make every effort to achieve some degree of clarity in our ideas; here is some advice which is entirely practical. As the general plan is usually carried out step by step, and as an attack is developed in successive waves, so can we make our task easier by concentrating in turns on immediate objects, such as the occupation of a certain square, the opening of a line, pinning a piece or exchanging another, etc. The basic plan, however, must be there, for, otherwise, how could these various manœuvres benefit us ? Matters are easier when, having the advantage, we are fully aware of the location and extent of a weakness in the hostile camp. It is then, in the main, a case of deciding on what means to employ in order to reach and to undermine it.

Besides ordinary attacking manœuvres there are other means of establishing and increasing an advantage, namely, combinations or, conversely, simplification of a position by exchanging material; but these must be looked upon as special cases. We must not forget the transition into the end game, of which we have already spoken. This is of particular moment when, in the middle game, our position can be threatened in spite of our advantage. Moreover, an advantage (say of a pawn) is, in the nature of things, useless in the middle game, but of the greatest value in an end game. Bearing in mind all we have said on the subject, it is important that the entry into the end game stage should be deliberate and at the free will of the player who has the advantage and to whom it will be profitable, and not merely a fortuitous happening or a disagreeable surprise, by which the advantage disappears or loses all significance. The average player is prone to saying, "It had to be," "It so happened"—he should be able to say, "I willed it," "It is done."

(a) The Attack

Methods of attack are numerous and varied; we could hardly enumerate them all. A separate book on the subject would be needed to study them in detail. It is sufficient for our purpose to recall their essential characteristics.

As the most decisive and interesting attacks are those

which are directed against the King, it makes a vast difference whether the King is in the centre or on one of the wings. It makes little difference, comparatively speaking, whether the King has castled on the K side or on the Q side. But his position in the centre is always hazardous, until he can escape into safety on one of the wings. The attacker has therefore an interest in keeping the hostile King in the centre, for once he has castled he is comparatively safe; there is, at any rate, no safer place. The pawns, too, are treated differently according to whether the King is attacked in the centre or on the flank. The centre pawns are, as a general rule, advanced, and will have to be exchanged in order to open the files for the Rooks. The wing pawns, on the contrary, are mostly on their original squares and can be either disregarded or used actively in an assault.

We have here a second basic difference: the pawns can take an active part in the attack or the attack can be carried out entirely by pieces. The latter is only successful if our pieces in the critical sector are more numerous than the opponent's, in fact, so much so that, in addition to overcoming the resistance of the defending pieces, they can also cope with the pawns which protect the position.

Where the attacker's pawns play an active rôle they must be thrown forward ruthlessly against the hostile position: they drive back on their way all the defender's pieces and destroy the hostile barrier of pawns, giving themselves up in order to open the way for the attacker's pieces, which would otherwise remain masked.

The few examples shown hereafter will elucidate these various forms of attack.

In Diag. 41 White is conducting a K side attack and

Black is attacking on the Q side. White's is a mating attack, which is *ipso facto* of greater importance, and

DIAGRAM 41

White: Forgacz; *Black:* Tartakower
St. Petersburg, 1909

sacrifices are indicated in order to bring it to a successful end. White's position appears to be admirable and full of promise, but his pawn-chain keeps all lines closed so that his pieces cannot take an effective part in the attack. On the other hand, Black's pawn-formation is in no way weakened and his inferiority really lies in the absence of defending pieces near the King's field. It follows therefore that White must by some means force through some of his pieces for the attack in order to decide the issue. Any loss of time, however, would give Black the chance of consolidating his position by ... P—B 4; and ... P—Kt 3; after which the Q R, placed at Q R 2, could participate in the defence of the K side.

Energetic action is therefore an urgent necessity.

1	P—B 5	K P × P
2	P—Kt 4	B P × P
3	Kt—Kt 5	

This manœuvre provokes a weakening of Black's pawn position. If ... P—R 3; 4 Kt—R 7, and after the Rook has moved out of danger, 5 Kt—B 6 *ch*, etc.

3	...	P—Kt 3
4	R—B 6	

White forthwith occupies the newly-created "hole" with a fourfold threat to Black's K B P as well as a threat of Kt × R P, in co-operation with the Queen.

4	...	K—Kt 2
5	Q R—K B 1	B—K 1
6	Q—B 4	Kt—Q 1
7	P—K 6	

A third pawn is offered in sacrifice, but it evidently cannot be taken. The white pieces are perfectly safe on the black squares.

7	...	R—R 3
8	Q—K 5	K—R 3
9	Q R—B 5	B P × P
10	Kt—B 7 *ch*	Q × Kt
11	R—R 5 *ch*	K—Kt 2
12	R × P *mate*	

Let us now examine a position (Diag. 42) in which the pawns take an active part in the attack. Here White has only three pieces available to carry out the necessary manœuvre, but he has four pawns to two on the K side, where, moreover, Black's pawn position is weakened. There are Bishops of opposite colours, so that on black squares Black's pawns are invulnerable. The task of eliminating Black's Bishop falls to the white pawns which are moving up to the assault. The K B P must move to B 6, and the breaking up of the adverse K side pawns must therefore be left to the K R P.

DIAGRAM 42

White: Tarrasch; *Black:* Schlechter
Match, 1911

1	P—Kt 4	R—K B 1
2	P—Kt 5	B—Kt 2
3	K—Kt 3	

A subtle move with a twofold object: to protect the
K B P, and to promote the advance of the K R P, without
Black's Queen being able to reach her K Kt 5. It is,
however, a mistake, as Black could obtain a draw by
perpetual check as follows: 3 ... R × P; 4 K × R, B—
K 4 *ch*; etc. This is a striking example of the neglect
of a tactical chance.

3   ...   Q—R 2

A bad move which leaves the Queen far away from
the main battlefield. At Q 2 she retained the option of
supporting the advance at an opportune moment of the
Q P or, alternatively, she would even be better placed
at K 1, from where a check at K 4 would be threatened
after White's P—B 5.

There is, however, no good move against the avalanche

of pawns; any move would have been immediately refuted.

    4 R—B 1   P—R 3

The object of this move is not the opening of the K R file, for in inferior positions it is in the highest degree unwise for the defender to allow the opening of lines. But in this case, were White to take the R P, Black's Bishop would recapture and get back into play; White's strategy would be set at naught. By the advance in the text Black desired rather to close the K R file against the advance of White's K R P. The drawback is that Black's K Kt P is now weak and unprotected.

    5 P—R 4   P—R 4

Now the advance of White's K B P is assured.

    6 P—B 5   P × P

    7 P × P   R—K 1

Although ... B—K4 *ch*; liberated the Bishop, it was no better than the text-move, as the R P cannot be defended.

    8 P—B 6   B × P

If ... R—K 6 *ch*; 9 Q × R, P × Q; 10 R—B 8 *ch*, followed by B—B 2, and mate. A simple strategic combination.

    9 P × B   Q—Q 2

Here again ... R—K 6 *ch*; was not feasible because of the same sacrifice, with mate one move later.

    10 Q—Kt 6   Resigns.

Where pawns take no active part in the attack, the heavy task of bearing the brunt of the contest devolves on the pieces, which must weaken the enemy position and prepare the decisive action.

This type of attack is far more difficult to conduct, but also less hazardous, than when pawns are in co-operation, because manœuvres by pieces do not weaken

a position in the same permanent manner as does an
advance by pawns. The position in Diag. 43 is of
particular interest, because the two Knights are the most

DIAGRAM 43

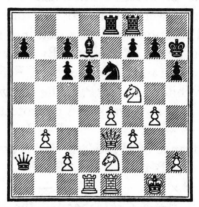

White: Capablanca; *Black:* Bernstein
San Sebastian, 1911

active pieces, and an attack by two Knights, practically
unsupported, is something of a rarity.

There are already some weaknesses in the black camp,
particularly the K Kt P and K R P and the square at
K Kt 4. All these weaknesses are on black squares,
which are controlled by the white Queen supported by
the two Knights, standing, of course, on white squares.
A fresh attack on the K Kt P would jeopardise Black's
game for this pawn cannot advance as the K R P is
attacked, and if it is captured, Black's K B 3 would very
soon be occupied by a white Knight.

   1 Kt (K 2)—Kt 3 Q × B P

Threatening the exchange of Queens by ... Q—B 4.

   2 R—Q B 1 Q—Kt 7

Hoping to use the Queen for the defence of K Kt 2

and of the black squares on the K side generally, which White at once prevents.

3	Kt—R 5	R—K R 1
4	R—K 2	Q—K 4
5	P—B 4	Q—Kt 4
6	Kt (B 5) × Kt P	

Threatening to win the exchange. The Knight cannot be captured because of 7 Kt—B 6 *ch*. If 6 ... R—Q 1; 7 Kt × Kt, and there is no defence against Q—Q 4, or Q—Q B 3. The black-square policy triumphs.

6	...	Kt—B 4
7	Kt × R	B × Kt
8	Q—Q B 3	P—B 3
9	Kt × P *ch* and wins.	

Pieces as well as pawns can be sacrificed in order to disrupt the hostile position, but this can only happen when there is an overwhelming superiority of available attacking over defending pieces. In such cases there will be an adequate number of pieces left to enforce a mate, provided they have sufficiently rapid access to the hostile K position.

The position is Diag. 44 is too well known to require any comment. It will be sufficient to quote the moves of this brilliant combination, which is the prototype of others of the same kind.

1	B × P *ch*	K × B
2	Q × Kt *ch*	K—Kt 1
3	B × P	K × B
4	Q—Kt 4 *ch*	K—R 2
5	R—B 3	P—K 4
6	R—R 3 *ch*	Q—R 3
7	R × Q *ch*	K × R
8	Q—Q 7 and wins.	

DIAGRAM 44

White: Lasker; *Black:* Bauer
Amsterdam, 1889

Attacks in the centre are no less interesting, although, as a rule, they are easier to handle. Examine Diag. 45. The essentials of the position are as follows :

Black's King is still on his original square in the

DIAGRAM 45

White: Spielmann; *Black:* Réti
Abbazia, 1912

centre. His Q P is the mainstay of his defence; were it
to fall, then the white centre pawns would decide the
game. Black's King might save himself by castling on
the Q side: this must be prevented. Before he can
castle, the Q B must move, for preference to K 3 in order
to support the Q P: this move must also be prevented
or at least its execution must be made difficult.

To sum up, the objective is the advance of the central
pawns and the opening of the centre files facing the
King, and the means to this end are the open Q Kt file
and the Bishops' diagonals.

1	R—Kt 1	Kt—Q 1
2	P—B 4	B—K 3
3	Kt—K 3	P × P

If instead of this move Black were to protect his Q P
by 3 ... P—Q B 3; White would exchange pawns and
renew the attack with the pawn now at Q B 2. He
would in any event obtain an open diagonal for an attack
on the King by B—Q Kt 5.

4   B—K 4

Not only attacking the Q Kt P, but threatening to
advance the Q P, attacking the B, which being at
last developed, becomes a target for the white forces.

4   ...   P—Q B 3

5   P—Q 5

Here White could have sacrificed the exchange with
5 R × P, with an easy win.

5   ...   B—Q B 4

Prolonging the agony by the sacrifice of a piece.

6	K—R 1	B × Kt
7	P × B	Kt × P

White threatened Q—Q 7 *ch.*

8	B × B	Q × P

9	B × K R P	R—R 1
10	K R × P	R—Q 1
11	Q × Kt P	Q × B
12	B—Kt 6 and wins.	

All these attacking manœuvres are comparatively simple. There are far more complicated examples, in which the play is extremely difficult, and where the basic plan, aiming at the break-up of the defence, requires minute investigation. A continuous search for new tactical points is necessary and advantage must be taken of every opportunity and of every weakness in the enemy camp, in order to increase the pressure.

The following example (Diag. 46) is much more complex.

The chief points to be noticed are: the open K R file, the weakened diagonal Q R 2—K Kt 8, and the Kt at K B 5. By forcing the exchange of Black's Q B, White weakens the whole of the white squares in the enemy camp and

DIAGRAM 46

White: Capablanca; *Black:* Marshall
Match, 1909

establishes his Queen there. Together with the pressure on two open lines this is sufficient to win.

1	Q—K 3	P—B 3
2	B—R 4	Kt—K 2
3	B—Kt 3	P—B 3
4	Q—Kt 3	P—R 4

The object of this move is not an attack on White's K B but the defence of the K side by the Q R from Q R 2. For this purpose the second rank must be cleared of all forces.

5	P—R 4	Kt—B 2
6	B—K 3	P—Kt 3
7	R—R 4	K—B 1
8	Q R—R 1	Kt—Kt 1

White has reached the desired position. Nearly all his pieces can participate in the attack. It is now a question of breaking down Black's power of resistance by forcing the exchange of his Bishop, and by bringing into active play his own Q B, which hitherto held only a watching brief.

9	Q—B 3	B × Kt
10	Kt P × B	R—Q 3
11	Q—R 5	R—R 2
12	Q—Kt 6	

With the elimination of Black's Bishop the white squares have become weak and are at once occupied by enemy forces. Now White threatens R—R 7.

12	...	Kt (B 2)—R 3
13	R × Kt	P × R
14	B × P *ch*	

By sacrificing the exchange White has brought his Q B into active play; now his superiority in material becomes overwhelming.

14	...	K—K 2
15	Q—R 7 *ch*	K—K1
16	Q × Kt *ch*	K—Q 2
17	Q—R 7 *ch*	Q—K 2
18	B—B 8	Q × Q
19	R × Q *ch*	K—K 1
20	R × R	Resigns

Still more difficult is the attack when conducted, not as here, in one particular quarter, but over the whole board. But the example shown in Diag. 47 is sufficiently complicated. It shows an attack on the King's field combined with pressure in the centre. As in the other examples the essentials are: the opening of lines and the creation of strong points. Note, for instance, how White opens here two lines for his K R and Q B: the K B file and the diagonal Q B 1 to K R 6. Then observe how he creates strong squares at Q 6 and Q B 4, to which is added shortly after K B 5, all of which are occupied successively by the Knights. White's task was made

DIAGRAM 47

White: Botvinnik; *Black:* Tartakower
Nottingham, 1936

easier by the fact that Black had weakened his K side
by ... P—K Kt 4; but this advance was made in answer
to White's threat of P—K B 4, which is precisely the
manner in which a weakness should be exploited in the
course of an attack.

1	P—B 4	Kt P × P
2	Kt P × P	K—Kt 2
3	P × K P	Q P × P
4	P—B 5	P × P
5	Kt × P	Q—B 3
6	Kt—Q B 4	Kt—Kt 3
7	Kt—Q 6	

This Kt cannot be captured because of 8 Kt × Kt,
winning a piece. The whole of White's manœuvre was
carried out with the utmost precision and dispatch.

7	...	B—K 3
8	Kt × B	

White disdains to win the exchange ; he is playing for
a mate.

8	...	Kt × Kt
9	R × Kt	

And now it is White who gives up the exchange. Black's
King is deprived of all defending forces and the white
pieces, Q, R, B and Kt, force the win.

9	...	K × R
10	Q—R 5	

An important move which not only threatens Q ×
R P *ch*, and B—Kt 5 *mate*, but clears the way for the
remaining Rook. Black is unable to guard the K R P
because of R—B 1 *ch*, and the B P falls.

10	...	Kt—Kt 3
11	Kt—B 5	R—K Kt 1

The Kt could not be taken because 11 ... B × Kt;
12 P × B, attacks the Queen.

| | 12 | Q × P | B × P |
| | 13 | R—Q 1 | |

Suddenly, and rather unexpectedly, the open Q file
decides the game. But at this stage White could win
in one of several ways.

	13	...	Q R—Q 1
	14	Q—Kt 5 *ch*	K—K 3
	15	R × R	P—B 3
	16	R × R	Kt—B 5
	17	Q—Kt 7	Resigns.

Finally we shall give an even more complicated
example (Diag. 48). The striking feature in this position
is that, at the moment, there is no sign of an attack.
It must be created in every particular. When it is
launched the adversary is not reduced to a passive
defence; on the contrary he initiates counter-attacks on
the other wing. In this way Black must conduct his

DIAGRAM 48

White: Alekhine; *Black:* Levitzki
Vilna, 1912

attack, and at the same time ward off his opponent's assaults in another sector.

Let us see, first of all, how Black assumes the initiative by paralysing the enemy forces.

       1 ...   Kt × Kt

Clearing the way for his K B P.

       2 B × Kt   Kt—Q 5

Attacking White's K P.

       3 Q—Q 1   B—K Kt 5

Again attacking the same pawn.

       4 R—K 1

The white K B P has now become weak; a target for Black's concentrated attack.

       4 ...   P—Q B 3

To enable the K B P to advance.

       5 B—Kt 2   P—B 4

Threatening ... P—B 5; opening the K B file, with an attack by the Rook on White's K B P.

       6 P—R 3   B—R 4
       7 P—Q Kt 4   B—R 2
       8 Kt—Kt 3   P—B 5
       9 P—Kt 4

Closing the diagonal for the Bishop, without opening the file for the Rook. But it creates a fresh weakness and allows the adverse Queen to participate in the attack.

       9 ...   Q—R 5
     10 P—B 5

Closing the diagonal of another Bishop. The battle rages round open lines.

     10 ...   Kt × Kt
     11 Q × Kt *ch*   B—B 2

The Bishop has retired without losing a *tempo* and now threatens to take part in the attack on another diagonal.

12   Q—B 3

The Q B P must be protected.

12   ...   P—K R 4

A new wave in the attack. If White captures the
pawn the Bishop will again come into its own and ...
P—B 6; will be threatened. On the other hand, the
K Kt P cannot be guarded. Therefore White takes
measures for bringing the Queen to the K side for
defensive purposes.

13   P—Q 4   R P × P

Black, of course, refrains from capturing the Q P, as
then White would have an excellent diagonal Q R 1—
K Kt 7 and would threaten the K B P.

14   R P × P   B—Q 4

Better than ... Q × P; after which White could still
hold the position by Q P × P, P—B 3, etc. As it is
the only piece which protects White's King is eliminated.

15   Q P × P   B × B
16   K × B   Q × Kt P *ch*
17   K—B 1   P × B P

Threatening to advance this pawn, thus opening a
diagonal for the Bishop.

18   P × P   B × P
19   Q × B   Q—R 6 *ch*
20   K—Kt 1   R—B 4
21   Q—B 4 *ch*   K—R 1

White is lost. He is threatened with mate or the
doubling of the black Rooks. If 22 B × P, Q—Kt 5 *ch*;
winning the Bishop.

22   Q × K B P   R × Q
23   B × R   R—K B 1 and wins.

(*b*) *Manœuvring*

In manifestly superior positions an attack at times is

impossible, because the advantage is not sufficiently great, or because a possible objective is not important enough or, again, because the necessary forces are not available. Frequently, also, the characteristics of a position are not favourable for an attack; closed positions are seldom subjected to a lively attack. For that reason we often find the initial stage of the middle game taken up by preparatory manœuvres. This happens, for instance, immediately after the opening, when positions are equal, before the balance between the two parties has been disturbed.

As at present we are dealing with positions in which one side has a certain advantage, the particular question to be answered is: how can we exploit and increase our advantage when for one reason or another an attack is not possible?

It requires a far more subtle and difficult method than a mere attack, and that for several reasons. First of all, in an attack, the target is much more obvious, and, in consequence, it is much easier to decide where to place our forces, and which particular units are indispensable. Furthermore, the means of conducting an attack are well known: opening lines, breaking up a pawn-chain, throwing our pawns forward for the assault, and concentrating our forces on an obvious weakness. Finally, threats are much more direct and the defensive possibilities more easily seen.

The first difficulty arising from this type of manœuvres is that the opponent has such a great number of possible replies that it is impossible to foresee even his next move. In order not to lose our way in a multitude of variations, we must, as far as possible, have the clearest conception of what we want to achieve. A general

notion would not suffice. As a starting point, we must
first find out in what our superiority consists, and then
where our opponent's real weakness is to be found. It
is far better to have a restricted but well-defined objective,
e.g., creation and occupation of a strong point, the
besieging of a weak square in the adversary's camp, the
opening of a file, etc., etc., than to wallow in a maze of
generalities, without any fixed purpose. The real difficulty will be found in even and well-balanced positions;
where an advantage exists, it is only a question of careful,
persevering play, in order to see the objective in a clear
light, as well as the means of reaching it.

We shall first examine a very simple illustration
(Diag. 49). Here Black has a backward pawn on an

DIAGRAM 49

White: Botvinnik; *Black:* Capablanca
Moscow, 1936

open file; this is his weakness, and here White's advantage is to be found. He will concentrate all his forces
against this pawn, and, in the first place, prevent its
advance. This is of great importance, for this advance,

although it would not prevent future attacks, would at once give the black pieces their freedom of action. As it is, all the black pieces will remain confined to two ranks for the protection of this important pawn. However, as the pawn can be defended as many times as it can be attacked, how can White increase his advantage? The fact that the said advantage is one of space provides the answer. White must not look for threats; rather must he seek to restrict his opponent more and more and, in the end, force his pieces more or less into a position of stalemate.

1	P—K 4	Q R—Q 1
2	Q R—Q 1	Q—Kt 2
3	P—B 3	Kt—K 1
4	R—Q 2	P—B 4
5	K R—Q 1	B—Kt 4

The pawn cannot be taken: 5 ... P × P; 6 Q × K P, Q × Q; 7 Kt × Q, P—Q 3; 8 B—R 3.

6	R—Q 3	B—B 3
7	P—K 5	B—K 2
8	Q—B 2	

In order to place the Queen behind a Rook.

8	...	R—B 2
9	Q—Q 2	B—Kt 5
10	P—Q R 3	B—B 1

By 10 ... B × Kt; Black would lose his only active piece. Sooner or later the white Bishop would attack the Q R, and the Q P would fall.

11	Kt—K 2	Kt—B 2
12	Kt—B 4	P—Kt 3
13	P—K R 4	P—Q Kt 4

Black is choking; he now tries a diversion, which costs him a pawn but affords a little breathing space.

The logical continuation would have been 13 ... B—R 3; but White could win a pawn by the following combination: 14 Kt × K P, B × Q; (14 ... Kt × Kt; 15 Q × B,) 15 Kt × R, Q any; 16 Kt × R, K × Kt; 17 R × B, and the Q P can no longer be defended.

       14   P × P   Q × P

If 14 ... Kt × P; 15 Kt × K P.

       15   R—Q B 1   Q—Kt 2

The Knight cannot move away because Kt × P, would again be threatened. The reason is now clear why this Knight moved to K B 4: with a R at Black's Q 1 the Q P is pinned and the K P has also become weak and insufficiently protected.

       16   R × Kt

This wins a pawn and thereby the game. White's strategy is thus justified. But it might possibly have been better for White to keep up the pressure, instead of being content with a small gain in material. By playing 16 Q—R 5, and after 16 ... R—B 1; 17 R (Q 3) —B 3, White would have forced his opponent to resign.

       16   ...   Q × R
       17   Kt × K P   P × Kt
       18   R × R, etc.

The last example showed how to take advantage of an open file. The next example, also a simple one, illustrates the exploitation of strong squares (Diag. 50).

Having weakened the black squares on Black's K side by the advance of his K R P, White has created some very strong points at K 5 and Q B 5. He is now bent on occupying them. A K side attack seems called for, and many players in this position would have unhesitatingly embarked upon it. But in that case Black would obtain counter-chances on the Q side, after occupying a

White: Alekhine; *Black:* Rubinstein
The Hague, 1921

strong square at his K B 4 and making full use of the open Q B file.

1	Kt—B 1	R—B 2
2	Kt—Kt 3	Kt—R 4
3	Kt—B 5	Kt—B 5

The Knight could not be taken because of 3 ... B × Kt; 4 P × B, Q × P; 5 B—Q 4, Q—B 3; 6 Kt—K 5, Q any; 7 Kt—Kt 4, threatening Kt—B 6 *ch*, and the attack against the King comes into being. How many attacks there are on various parts of the board ! This is great Chess !

4	K B × Kt	P × B
5	Kt—K 5	

Now White attacks the Bishop twice and the pawn at B 5 at the same time. If ... B × Kt (B 4); a piece is lost after P × B.

5	...	B × Kt (K 4)
6	B × Kt	B—Q 3

If 6 ... R—K 1; White continues 7 P×B, R×B;
8 Kt—K 4, with the double threat of Kt—B 6 *ch*, and
Q—Q 6.

7	B×R	B×B
8	Kt×B	R×Kt

And White wins, being the exchange ahead.

The following example (Diag. 51) is more complex
and, at the same time, very beautiful; it is positional play
of the highest class. It could serve as an object lesson
in the intermediary phase between the opening and the
middle game as well as in the treatment of an advantage
in space. It is quite clear that such an advantage exists
here, and it will occasion no surprise to see the attacker

DIAGRAM 51

White: Botvinnik; *Black:* Flohr
Moscow, 1936

proceed slowly and without direct threats. It will require
a good deal of time to increase this small advantage and
to bring the game to a successful issue.

    1   R—B 3

A simple warning that Black may, after all, have to

face an attack, which warning Black cannot disregard.
But White's real intention is to double his Rooks and
to operate in the centre.

	1	...	Q—K 1
	2	R—Q 1	R—Q 1
	3	P—Q Kt 3	

White liberates his Queen ; there are now, in fact,
possibilities of attack.

	3	...	P—K B 4
	4	Kt—Q 3	

He now avoids an exchange of Knights which would
close the K file for him. Only when the Q file is in his
entire control will he submit to this exchange.

	4	...	B—B 3
	5	B—B 2	Q—B 2
	6	Kt—K 1	K R—K 1
	7	K R—Q 3	

The manœuvre, which was begun at move 1, is now
accomplished. The Rooks are doubled on the Q file.

	7	...	Kt—K B 1
	8	Kt—B 3	Q—B 2
	9	Kt—K 5	

The Knight's manœuvre is picturesque; it has taken
four moves and completed a full circle, only to return
to the square from which it started ! But now Black
cannot very well exchange it, as White would then
obtain permanent mastery of the Q file.

	9	...	Kt (Kt 3)—Q 2
	10	Q—Q 2	B—K 2

Now Black again threatens to exchange Knights,

	11	Kt—B 3	Kt—B 3

and at the same time he has opened the way to his K 5
for his own Knight.

12	Q—B 1	Kt—K 5
13	Kt—K 5	Kt × B
14	K × Kt	Kt—Q 2
15	Q—K 3	Kt × Kt

Now that White can no longer monopolize the Q file
Black exchanges the terrible white Knight.

16	B P × Kt	Q—R 4
17	P—Q R 4	R—Q 2
18	P—Kt 3	Q—Q 1
19	K—Kt 2	B—Kt 4
20	Q—B 3	Q—K 2
21	P—B 5	

White's plan seemed to be to advance the Q P, and
Black was chiefly concerned in preparing for that eventuality. But now White embarks upon another scheme,
which would not have been feasible had Black still possessed
a Knight (a black Knight posted at its Q 4 would have
been too powerful a weapon). With the text-move
White threatens P—Q Kt 4—5. Black will parry this
advance but another threat will arise—the posting of
the white Knight at Q 6.

21	...	P—Q R 4
22	Kt—Kt 1	Q—B 1
23	Kt—R 3	B—Q 1
24	Kt—B 4	B—B 2
25	Kt—Q 6	

Another wondrous journey by the Knight, from Q B 3
to Q 6 in four moves !

25	...	R—Kt 1
26	R—Q Kt 1	

Threatening P—Q Kt 4. Black always manages to
find defensive moves which enable him just to hold
the position. But moves are getting scarce for him.

26	...	Q—Q 1
27	P—Q Kt 4	P × P
28	R × P	B × Kt

The only way to preserve the Q Kt P.

29	K P × B

Note that all pawn captures are made towards the Queen's wing, whilst the K side is neglected. This shows a true insight into the position.

29	...	Q—R 4
30	R (Q 3)—Kt 3	R—K 1
31	Q—K 2	Q—R 1

White's threat is Q—B 4, R—Kt 6, Q—Kt 4, winning a pawn.

32	R—K 3	K—B 2
33	Q—B 4	

Now that White has more or less a won game he makes a slight error, which affords his opponent an unexpected tactical opportunity. A striking demonstration of the necessity for constant and unremitting attention !

33	...	P—Q Kt 4

This pawn cannot be captured because of 34 ... P × P *dis. ch.*; winning the Queen. Thus Black gets rid of his weak and backward Q Kt P.

34	Q—B 2	R × P

Black thinks that, thanks to his opponent's slight error, he can relieve the pressure by combinative play. A little better would be 34 ... R—R 2; although in that case White has a combination, as follows: 35 P—Q 5, and if ... B P × P; 36 R × Kt P, or if 35 ... K P × P; 36 Q × P *ch.*

35	P × R	P—B 4 *dis. ch*

It is clear that on his 33rd move White should first

have moved his King away from the diagonal and from
the distant threat by Black's Queen.

36   K—R 3   P × R
37   Q—B 7 *ch*   K—Kt 1
38   P—Q 7 and wins.

The connoisseur will realise how much more there is
in play of this type than in a simple, if brilliant, combination. The student who has studied this game with
sufficient care will grasp not only the sense of each
individual move, but that of the various series of manœuvres. He will find himself the better armed for his own
struggles.

(c) *Bringing about an End Game*

We have already examined some examples of the
transition from the middle game into the end game.
It must always be borne in mind that this transition
frequently provides a method of accentuating some advantages which are of little value in the middle game.
Again, in the middle game, we might, even with a
numerical advantage, be faced with a loss owing to
positional considerations; if we can then bring about
an end game, we can make the most of our extra material,
provided always that we are sufficiently familiar with end
game conditions, to know whether this change in any
particular case is desirable or not.

In the position shown in Diag. 52 White has a substantial advantage in all three elements, while Black
occupies the open K B file with his heavy artillery and
threatens the K B P. Its protection would keep the
whole of the White forces tied up. White's real advantage consists in an extra pawn, the Q P, which is backward
and cannot be exploited in the middle game. If White

DIAGRAM 52

White: Tchigorin; *Black:* Blackburne
Hastings, 1895

could only lead into an end game he could easily make
the most of this pawn and with Bishops of the same
colour, and Black's Q side pawns of the same colour as
the Bishop, victory would presumably be his. It is not
surprising, therefore, to see White making a series of
exchanges in order to bring about the end game. His
method is one of direct threats, but one could imagine
another procedure: that of gradually warding off the
enemy attack, making all possible exchanges in the process.

1	P—B 4	Q—B 3 *ch*
2	Q—B 3	Q × Q *ch*
3	K × Q	R—Q 1

If 3 ... P × P; the white Bishop's long diagonal and
the K file are opened simultaneously, which gives White
the opportunity of a decisive attack: 4 R—K 7 (threatening R × B, and B × P *ch*), P × P *dis. ch* ; 5 K—Kt 2,
R—B 7 *ch*; 6 K—Kt 1, B—Q 1 ; 7 B × P *ch*, winning
the exchange.

4   B × P

More decisive perhaps would be 4 K—K 4.

4	...	B × B
5	R × B	R × Q P *ch*
6	R (K 1)—K 3	R × R *ch*
7	K × R	R—B 1
8	R—K 6	R—Q Kt 1
9	K—K 4	

and the win for White is easy as, in addition to his extra pawn, his position is far superior, with the King in the centre and an active against a passive Rook.

In this example White, after the exchanges, has managed to maintain his advantage of one pawn; it is still more useful when the original advantage increases during the transition between middle and end game. Much more difficult, and not infrequent, are the cases in which the advantage held before the transformation changes in character or in value during this phase of the game. It is then a matter of careful judgment as to whether it is not better to cling to the existing advantage and to continue middle game play.

In Diag. 53 White has a marked advantage in time, having developed both his Knights whilst Black's K Kt has not moved yet, and his Q Kt is on an unfavourable square at Q R 3. In addition ... Castles K R; would take time, whilst ... Castles Q R; would cost a pawn. Black cannot drive off the advanced Knight by ... P—Q B 3; because of Kt—Q 6 *ch*. In the meantime White will play K R—K 1, and if Black replies ... Kt—K 2; the white King leaves the K file and the black Kt is pinned. If Black plays ... Kt—B 3; instead of ... Kt—K 2; again the white King leaves the K file, this time with check, and in moving out of check the black King will interrupt the connection between his

White: Tarrasch; *Black:* Mieses
Göteborg, 1920

Rooks. White's advantage thus appears to be overwhelming. But in one of the variations mentioned there is a *finesse*. If, after 1 ... Castles; White plays 2 Kt × P *ch*, the sequel is 2 ... K—Kt 1; 3 Kt (R 7)—Kt 5, P—Q B 3; and the Knight must move away from Q Kt 5 leaving his companion *en prise* by the Rook.

White must find a parry against this threat, otherwise Black can complete his development, and then White's advantage in time will have completely disappeared. As we know, an advantage in time cannot be maintained except by constant threats. Now is the crucial moment: White has reached the peak of his advantage, and, unless he finds "something," he will begin going downhill. This is also the time to exchange the advantage in time for one in another element, or, alternatively, to try to reach the end game stage. The game continued as follows: 1 K R—K 1, Castles; 2 Kt × P *ch*, K—Kt 1; 3 Kt (R 7)—B 6 *ch*, P × Kt; 4 Kt × P *ch*, K—B 1; 5 Kt × R, K × Kt; and we have reached an ending in which White has a

Rook and two united passed pawns against two Knights;
is it enough to win ? Probably it is (in the actual game
White won). But the original advantage was very small,
and ordinarily, after these exchanges, a win for White
could not be guaranteed.

Diag. 54 illustrates another case of the same kind.
Black has an extra pawn whilst his opponent has a fairly
strong attack; he naturally desires to bring about an
end game as quickly as possible, in which his advantage
will be of greater effective value. But he cannot achieve

DIAGRAM 54

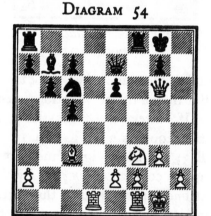

White: Euwe; *Black:* Alekhine
Match, 1935

this end without losing his extra pawn. Where, then, will
be his advantage ? He therefore formulates a plan in
which the sacrifice of his pawn will lead to an end game
which, positionally, is won for him. This kind of play
obviously requires a profound knowledge of the end
game and the faculty to visualize the desired position
many moves ahead.

1	...	Q—B 2
2	Q—Kt 5	Q R—Q 1

3	P—K R 4	R × R
4	R × R	Kt—Q 5

This is the pawn-sacrifice which enforces the exchange of all the pieces.

5	B × Kt	P × B
6	R × P	B × Kt
7	R—K B 4	Q—R 4
8	R × R *ch*	K × R
9	Q—B 4 *ch*	Q—B 2
10	Q × B	Q × Q
11	P × Q	P—K 4
12	K—B 1	P—Q Kt 4
13	K—K 2	

and now Black obtains a winning advantage by 13 ... P—R 4. In the actual game Black, feeling sure of a win, carelessly played ... P—B 4; and could only draw. It is a pity that such a deep plan should have been ruined by a simple oversight.

III. INFERIOR POSITIONS

1. Inferiority in Different Elements

The sagacious reader will wonder at the title of this division of the book, and, quite rightly, say that inferior positions can only be of the same types as those already examined, but seen from the opposite point of view. This is true and will enable us to restrict the number of examples, and much that has been said can serve us here. There is, nevertheless, a distinction: in many of the positions shown, the advantage led to victory because it was sufficiently big, or because the attack was conducted in superlative fashion, or finally, because the defender was not quite equal to his task. We shall now examine positions in which a disadvantage does not entail the loss of the game, because it is not important enough, or because the attacker failed to make the most of his chances or, finally, because the defender managed to discover unexpected resources.

One might suppose that all that has been said about superior positions would also apply to inferior ones, and the defender only needs to do the opposite of what the attacker was advised to do. There are, however, many points and problems which the defender has to think out and which are typical only of the defence; we shall elucidate them in the course of our explanations in connection with the positions illustrated and especially when we come to speak of "ideas in chess." We shall first examine the characteristics connected with the weaknesses in each element.

First of all there is inferiority in material, the simplest case, about which there is little to say.

Disadvantage in force does not necessarily mean the loss of a game; if it were so, no gambit, no combination would be playable.   But even if our opponent has actually won a piece or pawn otherwise than by an oversight on our part, he must have made some effort and spent some time in doing so.   There is, therefore, nearly always some compensation.   Psychologically, too, there is here a point to be considered: the player who, after sustained effort, has won some material, is naturally inclined to relax; having realised his intentions, he is not in the best condition for the immediate conception of another plan requiring further efforts.   This is the moment when we should try to assume the initiative and create as many difficulties for him as possible.   Passive acceptance of the situation almost certainly leads to disaster.

In Diag. 55 White has an advantage in material of Rook against Bishop and pawn.   In addition White threatens to initiate a K side attack.   What can Black do to counteract these unfavourable circumstances ?   Any

DIAGRAM 55

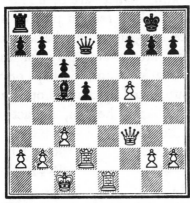

White: Mieses; *Black:* Capablanca
Berlin, 1913

plan likely to be suitable would try to utilise the extra pawn. But in an end game a Rook is more powerful than a Bishop and pawn, and so Black must avoid drifting into an ending and make the most of his extra pawn in the middle game, whilst warding off White's attack. Attack and defence are blended in his first move, which initiates Black's scheme.

1	...	B—K 2
2	Q R—K 2	B—B 3
3	Q—R 5	

A weak move. The Queen is now out of play. He should have continued his attack with P—K Kt 4, Q—Kt 3, P—K R 4, P—Kt 5, etc.

3	...	P—K R 3
4	P—K Kt 4	K—R 2

Because of the threat of P—K R 4, which now would be met by ... P—K Kt 3; winning the Queen. Thus Black has entirely safeguarded his position against any attack on the K side. He can now concentrate all his forces on the other wing and, with the white Queen out of play, his attacking chances are by no means negligible. Incidentally, for Black to remain passive would be most injudicious: once his Queen gets back into play, White could resume his attack and play for the end game. Four moves ago Black thought perhaps only of obtaining a passed pawn supported by the Bishop; but now, thanks to his opponent's lapse, he can, in fact he *must*, play for an energetic attack.

5	K—Kt 1	R—Q 1
6	R—Q 1	P—B 4
7	Q—R 3	Q—R 5

Black takes advantage of the fact that White has given up his attack against the K B P, in order to bring his

Queen into the game and to free his pawns for their advance. And so Black's Queen attacks the Q R and K Kt P, by which means the white Queen is still kept out of play.

        8   R (K 2)—Q 2   Q—K 5 *ch*
        9   K—R 1   P—Q Kt 4

The critical moment. Black could here obtain a passed pawn by 10 ... P—Q 5, which, at an earlier stage, would have satisfied his ambitions. But now he plays for more. As this move would have blocked his B, and the pawn would have easily been stopped by a hostile Rook, he makes use of all his resources and threatens ... P—Kt 5; which also would give him a passed pawn, without, however, blocking the Bishop.

        10   Q—Kt 2   Q—R 5
        11   K—Kt 1   P—Kt 5

We need go no further; it is clear that Black has now an active game and that his attack makes up for his material disadvantage; he has a considerable positional advantage, sufficient to win, which indeed he did after a short time.

Let us now examine the case of a disadvantage in space. Here it is of great importance to realise exactly in what our weakness consists, and what is our opponent's principal threat. Only then does it become possible to remedy the weakness and to parry the threat.

In the position shown in Diag. 56, which position also illustrates the transition from the opening into the middle game, Black has an advantage in space. Analysis will show us that White's weakness is his Q B which has hardly any scope. White would endanger his own position by P—K 4, as Black's answer ... Kt—K 4; in connection with ... Kt—B 5 ; aiming at both the B and

DIAGRAM 56

White: Tarrasch; *Black:* Duras
Hamburg, 1910

the Q Kt P, is perhaps his most serious threat.

    1   Kt—K 2

Threatening to develop the Bishop at Q B 3 and thereby to eliminate both his weaknesses at the same time, as the Q Kt P would then be protected.

    1   ...   P—Kt 5

To prevent the manœuvre described above and also the minor threat of B—R 5. But the pawn itself is weakened by this advance as well as the square Q B 5 where a Knight might have been established.

    2   Kt (K 2)—Q 4   Kt—K 4

    3   Q—K 2

Preventing ... Kt—B 5; and indirectly protecting the Q Kt P. Black must bring up more pieces to accentuate the pressure.

    3   ...   Kt—K 5

    4   B—K 1

The Bishop is now still more restricted. But we now perceive White's intentions. As he could not open a diagonal for his Bishop by playing P—K 4, he now finds an opportunity of opening another diagonal by the advance of his K B P.

4	...	R—B 1
5	Q R—B 1	Kt—Q 3
6	Kt—Q 2	

A severe struggle is taking place for the control of Black's Q B 5.

| 6 | ... | B—B 3 |

Occupying the long diagonal with an attack on the Q Kt P.

| 7 | P—B 3 | |

At last this move has become possible. Now the strength of White's game lies in the position of the Knight at Q 4, from where it cannot be dislodged.

7	...	Kt—B 3
8	Kt × Kt	R × Kt
9	R × R	Q × R
10	Kt—Kt 3	

With a number of objects : defence of the Q Kt P, attack on the hostile Q Kt P, return of a Knight to Q 4.

| 10 | ... | Q—Kt 3 |
| 11 | B—B 2 | |

White's main object is achieved. His Bishop is developed and the positions have become equal. The game now proceeds towards a level ending.

11	...	Q—Kt 4
12	Q × Q	Kt × Q
13	R—Q 2, etc.	

It would be difficult to find a better illustration of the method of equalising a position against an advantage in space, an example the more instructive as such positions frequently occur after an indifferently played opening, with either Black or White at a disadvantage.   In similar cases every effort must be made to re-establish equality, without any thoughts of assuming the initiative; once that is achieved, and only then, can further plans be considered. The present game resulted in a draw. Dr. Tarrasch's final note to the game gives food for thought: "White thought his task well done, when he achieved equality in difficult circumstances and after a poor opening."

In this example, the difficulties of a disadvantage in space were overcome by a passive defence: this can, in rare cases, be effected by a counter-attack.

We shall now examine a position in which there is a disadvantage in time.

In Diag. 57 White has an advantage in space and in time, the latter being here of greater importance, as Black's Queen and K Rook are absent from the Q side, where an attack is in course of preparation. Black's first task, therefore, is to bring back these pieces with the utmost speed and, whilst holding off his opponent's

DIAGRAM 57

White: Capablanca; *Black:* Znosko-Borovsky
St. Petersburg, 1913

fast-developing attack, to prepare a counter-attack which, in the nature of things, must be launched in the centre.

1   B—B 3

Eliminating Black's vigorous Bishop, his best defensive unit, which incidentally creates weaknesses at Black's Q R 3 and Q B 3. Black, unable to prevent this, loses no time in recalling his troops.

1	...	K R—K 1
2	B × B	K × B
3	P—Q B 5	P—B 3

Preventing P—B 6 *ch.*

| 4 | Kt—B 3 | Q—B 1 |

Now Black's pieces are better placed; he has more space and has nearly caught up his adversary in point of time. But he still has weaknesses at Q 3 and on the Q B and Q R files. White's attack will develop here.

| 5 | Kt—Q 2 | P × P |

It is necessary to prevent White's Kt from reaching his Q 6.

| 6 | Kt—B 4 | Kt—Kt 3 |

With the same object. We see how Black guards his weakest point.

| 7 | Kt—R 5 *ch* | K—R 1 |
| 8 | P × P | |

If 8 Kt × P, then ... Kt—Q 4; and ... P—B 5. As we are dealing with the defence, we refrain from analysing all the attacking possibilities.

| 8 | ... | Kt—Q 4 |
| 9 | Q—Q 4 | R—B 1 |

Black has succeeded in guarding all his weak points and has reached equality in time. White is still ahead in space, but Black's Knight is very well posted in the centre. This is the critical moment, when an advantage in one element is converted into an advantage in another, or when the defender must consider the possibility of a counter-attack.

          10   P—B 4

Black's Knight at his Q 4 is the very basis of his defence; should it be dislodged, it would mean the total collapse of his strategy. This is the moment to start a counter-attack. Should it fail, the game is lost; but it would certainly also be lost were the Knight meekly to retire (Diag. 58).

DIAGRAM 58

10	...	P—K 4
11	Q—Kt 1	P—K 5

If the Rook moves away, Black plays ... P—K 6; threatening ... P—K 7; or better still ... Q × P. Therefore White decides to convert his advantage. He sacrifices the exchange in order to obtain a passed pawn; whether for attacking or defensive purposes is not quite clear.

12	P × Kt	P × R
13	P—Q 6	R—K 7

We can leave it at that: Black has succeeded not only

in eliminating his inferiority in time, but he has also found an adequate defence against White's attack. Moreover, he has won the exchange and, to set off against White's dangerous threat of P—Q 7, he has himself a few threats which cannot be disregarded.

We shall now leave the subject of the elements and pass on to the study of "ideas" in chess relating in the first place to inferior positions.

2. Various Means of Remedying Inferiority in Position

Once we have realised that our position is inferior, it is policy to ascertain whether our opponent's advantage is such that he can hope for an early win without having to resort to extreme measures. On the contrary, it may be his advantage is so minute that he must reckon with the probability of a long and arduous struggle in the course of which he must increase his advantage before he can think of forcing a win, or even that it will be necessary for him to rely on the end game.

Our strategy will depend on the nature of the answers to these questions. Although the player who has an advantage must himself know first of all what he wants, his opponent is reduced to guessing the attacker's intentions and plans. Yet it should be the motto of the defender not to submit to the will of the attacker but to escape his grip. Hence the necessity of being for ever on the look-out for chances of counter-attack. This is an even more pressing need when we are in real danger; there may lie our only salvation. If, on the contrary, our position shows no real weakness, we may rely on passive defence, in which, however, it should be our endeavour to keep engaged as many of the enemy pieces as possible, by which means we may obtain favourable opportunities. Every attack entails a certain amount of risk. It produces weaknesses at one point or another, especially in the case of pawns, or where there is a congestion of pieces on one particular part of the board; we must then bide our time. When the attack is beaten off, and the enemy's position is weakened and his pieces are ill-placed for the defence, then our chance will have come. It is in such cases that the ordinary precepts of sound defence are particularly valuable; the weaker party must not open lines, especially where his weakness lies, as it would only benefit his adversary. It is essential to ascertain whether the opponent is himself heedful of such precepts and whether he is not creating his own weaknesses. For instance, a flank-attack is not admissible unless the centre is blocked or at least strong. Any negligence in that respect must immediately be seized upon by the defender and exploited to the utmost.

A player, in an inferior position, would feel inclined at all times to follow a line of play entirely opposed to that which his opponent wishes to pursue. As his opponent is the stronger, it is not always possible and in any case would frequently help his intentions. A more subtle plan which, not infrequently, leads to success is to appear to acquiesce in the opponent's dictation. If he plays for an end game, allow him to obtain it, but try to find some *nuance* which will nullify his advantage. A purely psychological point arises here. By letting your opponent have his own way, you will probably make him think that your resistance has broken down and that you cannot hold him any more ; after his own efforts, he is the more likely to relax or, alternatively, to embark on risky adventures.

In an inferior position it is, in normal circumstances, futile to think of playing for a win before (and until) equality has been reached. But, in practice, it often happens that a player in an inferior position passes directly into one of decisive advantage, without going through an intermediate stage. This could result from a well-timed counter-attack, and also from opportunities which are apt to arise when the opponent is obstinately aggressive. A stubborn defence is likely to lure him on to undue commitments; even if he notices that his advantage is gradually disappearing it is too late to withdraw, and he drifts on until his game is lost.

Amongst the several means of counteracting an advantage in the hostile position the most usual are: passive resistance, counter-attack, and transition into the end game. Some special cases call for a number of exchanges and for cross-combinations. We shall examine them with the help of appropriate illustrations.

(a) Passive Defence

It is impossible to promulgate a hard and fast rule as to when a passive defence is to be preferred to a counter-attack; all that can be said is that passive resistance is called for when a counter-attack is either impossible or its preparation would require time. The two can of course be combined, nor is it rare for a passive defence to turn imperceptibly into a counter-attack. But the fact that you are reduced to a passive defence is no cause for despair; it works satisfactorily in an astonishingly large number of cases; the resources of the game are truly unending.

White, in the position shown in Diag. 59, has a splendid attacking game, marred only by the fact that

DIAGRAM 59

White: Alekhine; *Black:* Euwe
Match, Amsterdam, 1937

his K P is precariously posted at K 5. But his K side pawns threaten to advance *en masse* and, by opening files for his Rooks, to overcome the enemy's resistance. Black, for his part, has no opportunities at the moment for a counter-attack, as ... P—Q B 4; will not be playable for a long time to come, and would, at best, lead to the isolation of his Q P. Nevertheless, there is no weakness in his position, and this enables him to wait and, by a stubborn defence, lure into the attack the whole of White's forces, including his pawns. Once the attack is beaten off, the end game might prove unfavourable for White on account of the weakness of these pawns.

1	Kt—B 5	P—B 3
2	P—Kt 4	P × P
3	B × K P	Kt—B 3

It is clear that Black hopes to establish his Kt at his
K 5, from where it will exercise a strong pressure on
White's game, with a constant threat of ... Kt—B 7 *ch*.

    4 Q—Q 3   K—R 1

The last two moves foreshadowed the sacrifice by
White of his Kt for the K R P followed by Q—Kt 6 *ch*,
which Black immediately anticipates, by eliminating the
check.

      5 R—K Kt 1

Another, and more hazardous attack could be initiated
here by 5 P—Kt 5, with the sacrifice of a pawn.

      5 ...   B—B 2

With this move Black gives up any present intention
of advancing his Q B P ; he wishes to ease the pressure
by the exchange of his passive Bishop for the extremely
aggressive white Bishop.

      6 P—B 4

Again White could have tried a sudden onslaught by
6 P—Kt 5. The text move has the drawback that
Black can, though not on the next move, play his Knight
to his K 5.

      6 ...   Q—B 2

With a view to ... B × B; and ... Kt—K 5.

      7 Q R—K B 1

The sacrifice of the Knight at K Kt 7 leads to nothing
after ... R × B; and ... Kt—K 5.

      7 ...   B × B
      8 B P × B   Kt—K 5

After this move White's attack falls to pieces, and the
advantage passes to his opponent. The will to maintain
the attack at all hazards costs White the game.

      9 P—Kt 5

The sacrifice 9 Kt × R P, was unsound because of

9 ... Kt—B 7 *ch*; 10 K—Kt 2, R × Kt; 11 R × Kt,
R × P *ch*; etc.

9	...	P × P
10	Kt—Q 6	Kt—B 7 *ch*
11	K—Kt 2	Kt × Q
12	Kt × Q *ch*	K—Kt 1
13	Kt × P	R—Kt 3
14	P—K R 4	P—B 4

With this advance—the strategic turn which, from
the first, was pending—Black obtains the advantage.
Strategic objects and plans are, by their nature, permanent.   If only the player keeps them in mind they
will, at the proper moment and more often than not
unexpectedly, become practicable, with decisive results.

We shall now leave this position, in which the defence
has proved its worth with persuasive strength.

Here is another example of the same type (Diag. 60).
White threatens to attack the Q Kt P, which cannot
advance because it may then be attacked by the R P.

DIAGRAM 60

White: Köhnlein; *Black:* Tarrasch
Nuremberg, 1907

In addition he must safeguard his Queen which stands on the open Q Kt file. White will in any case prevent the Queen from reaching her Q R 4, pinning the Kt. Black's position looks precarious, in spite of his extra pawn. He has, however, some future hope of obtaining a favourable end game by ... P—K Kt 3; which would afford opportunities even in the middle game.

1	P—Q R 4	Q—Kt 5
2	P—R 5	K—Kt 1
3	K R—Q Kt 1	Q—B 4
4	Kt—R 4	Q—R 2

An unhappy position for a Queen, but Q 3 must remain free for the Knight.

5	P—B 4

Threatening to keep the Knight away from Black's Q 3 by P—B 5.

5	...	P—B 4
6	Kt—B 3	Kt—B 1
7	Kt—Q 5	Kt—Q 3

Black's object is achieved. He now threatens to drive away the white Knight and to win one of the pawns at White's Q B 4 and K 4. White immediately anticipates this threat.

8	K—B 3	P—B 3

Black is in a difficult situation. After this move he hopes to liberate his Queen, but his Q Kt 3 becomes weak and affords White the opportunity of an attack on his Q R P and Q B P.

9	Kt—Kt 6	K—B 2
10	R—Kt 1	

There was no necessity for transferring the attack to the other wing. He should have played Kt—R 4, threatening R—Kt 6, Q R—Q Kt 1, Kt × P, threatening Kt—K 6 *ch*, etc.

10	...	Q R—K Kt 1
11	Q—Q Kt 2	

March and counter-march ! He has lost a *tempo*: as the Queen cannot threaten Q Kt 6, only the attack on the Q B P remains.

11	...	Q—Kt 1
12	Kt—R 4	P—K Kt 3

With this move Black obtains chances on the other wing. Observe how many moves have been played before this advance has become feasible. What patience and what steadiness ! The main difficulty of such positions is that these purely human qualities are required rather than the genius of the chess-player.

13	Kt × P	Q—R 2
14	Q—R 3	P × P
15	Q R—Kt 1	

There was no objection to first recapturing the pawn.

15	...	P × P
16	Kt × Kt P	Kt × Kt
17	Q—K 7 *ch*	K—Kt 1
18	Q × B P	K—R 1
19	R × R *ch*	R × R
20	Q × B P	

Threatening R—Kt 6, and R × P. But Black has a defence, which will show that White's attack was conducted without sufficient care, in that he neglected his centre pawns.

20	...	P × P
21	R—Kt 6	P—Q 7
22	K × P	R—Q 1 *ch*
23	K—B 3	R—Q 3

24 Q—B 7   R × R
25 P × R   Q—Kt 1

Dr. Tarrasch rightly remarks that White, at this point, could still draw the game with P—B 5.

26 Q × R P   Kt—B 4

and Black won.

The next example (Diag. 61) will again emphasise the necessity, on the part of the defender, of thoroughly

DIAGRAM 61

White: Znosko-Borovsky; *Black:* Euwe
Broadstairs, 1921

understanding where his greatest weakness lies, for there the most dangerous attack is to be expected. Lacking this knowledge, he can hardly hope to defend himself successfully. He will find replies to immediate threats, but inevitably succumb to a long prepared *coup*, in the shape of an elaborate and lengthy attacking manœuvre.

In this position White has a substantial advantage and a strong attack against the hostile King. Black's pieces are unfavourably placed: his Bishops have no open diagonals, his Knight has no good square available. At the moment he has the choice of two moves: 1 ... P—B 5, by which he would obtain a majority of pawns on the Q side, and 1 ... P × P; winning a pawn, though a doubled one, and opening a diagonal for one of his Bishops. After this capture White's proper course is to refrain from recapturing the pawn, which would expose his pieces to pins, and to concentrate on the pawn at his Q 5, combined with an advance of his K Kt P, not omitting, of course, to withdraw his King from a possible check on the black diagonal.

1	...	P × P
2	Q—Kt 2	P—Q 6
3	K—R 1	

An important moment for Black. He must provide against White's numerous threats, the most important being the advance of the K Kt P and the attack on the pawn at Black's Q 4. He could parry this attack by giving up the exchange with ... R—B 5; but this sacrifice would only facilitate the advance of White's K Kt P. In addition White threatens to play Kt—Q 4, with an attack on the Q P: ... R—Q 3; 4 B—K B 4. If, in anticipation of this threat, he plays ... Kt—B 1; then 4 Kt—K 5, wins. He must therefore cope with this threat first of all, but, at the same time, he must foresee and provide against White's future threats. If, in order to prevent Kt—Q 4, he plays the obvious ... B—B 4; he relinquishes the control of his K Kt 5 which could be occupied by White's Knight, with a double threat (B and K R 7) and prospects of future attacks. This could be countered by ... Kt—B 3; but the Kt might be attacked and captured. He must therefore call upon another piece to protect the threatened squares.

It is now clear that the whole of Black's second rank

requires protection; the third rank is guarded by the
Rook at Q B 3, the first rank by the Queen; there
remains the second Rook to look after the second rank.
But to make this protection effective it becomes necessary
to clear the second rank of the pieces which at present are
encumbering it.   In this light all Black's moves are easily
understood.   In a previous example (Diag. 46) Black
effected the same defensive idea with a Rook at Q R 2, but
the idea underlying the attack ran on different lines, and so
the Rook at Q R 2 not only failed in its task but actually
caused the loss of the game, as it was deservedly captured.
In the present instance, matters are very different.   Black
has seen through White's intentions and arranges his
defence accordingly.

3	...	B—B 4
4	P—Kt 6	P × P
5	Kt—Kt 5	Kt—B 3
6	Kt × B	K × Kt
7	P × P *ch*	K—Kt 1
8	R × Kt	R × R
9	B × P *ch*	K—B 1
10	B—Kt 5	

As we are at present studying methods of defence, we
shall not pause to consider whether White has always
chosen the best moves.   For instance, here he could have
won a piece by simply playing 10 B × R, but Black
would have obtained a strong passed pawn after 10
... R—B 7; 11 B—Kt 5, R × Q; 12 B × Q, R × Q Kt P;
etc.   White hopes to do better by a direct attack.   His
idea is that, as the Q R has to move away, he can continue as follows : 11 B × R, P × B (if 11 ... Q × B;
12 R—K B 1, winning the Queen); 12 P—Kt 7 *ch*,
K—K 2; 13 P—Kt 8 (Q).   This is the combination

prepared by White 10 moves before. Has Black a valid defence against this threat?

         10   ...   R—R 2

Here it is. The Rook commands the whole of its second rank and prevents P—Kt 7. The third rank was guarded by a Rook. This barrier broke down; now Black has set up another and stronger one on the second rank. It provides a magnificent illustration of the defensive powers of a Rook, acting across the whole of the chessboard. Now White can do nothing better than win back the exchange, remaining with Bishops of opposite colours. A most instructive warning not to be content vaguely to say: "The piece I have attacked will have to move away somewhere," but to ascertain clearly where that somewhere might be. In attacking the Q R, White thought it would have to move somewhere, and left it at that. We have seen, on the contrary, that a well-thought-out retreat can be of inestimable value.

         11   B × R   P × B

The defence has succeeded brilliantly.

This closes the section on passive defence, and we shall now pass on to active defence, leading to the counter-attack.

(b) Counter-attack

We have stated that every defensive scheme should allow for a possible counter-attack, which must be prepared in good time. In order to be successful the basic object of a counter-attack, as well as the available means to carry it out, must be well understood. But the great difficulty is to gauge the right moment to launch such a counter-attack, and yet this is the most important point. A premature counter-attack is usually doomed to failure,

as is one which starts too late.   But when properly timed
and aimed at important objects with sufficient forces, it
frequently succeeds.

In Diag. 62, White has launched a powerful attack
against the hostile King.   The drawback in his position

DIAGRAM 62

White: Lasker; *Black:* Tarrasch
Match, 1908

is that he is unable to advance the K R P and K B P
with the required speed.   The B P in particular will be
troublesome, and the hostile Queen is on the same
diagonal, closed for the time being, but liable to be
opened at any moment.   Thus we discover the nucleus
of a counter-attack by Black.

1	P—Kt 4	P—Kt 3
2	Kt—R 6 *ch*	K—Kt 2
3	P—Kt 5	B—Q 1
4	Q—Kt 3	

With multiple threats—against the Kt, the Q P, the
Q R.   There is also the threatened transfer of the Q to
K R 6 *via* R 4.

4	...	P—B 3

Correct play ! Black not only defends himself, but he endeavours to open the K B file, which is bearing upon White's K B 2, the critical square against which Black's counter-attack is to be directed. If White defends himself by 5 P—K R 4, the continuation would be: 5 ... P × P; 6 P × P, R × B; 7 Q × R, B × P; and if 8 Q × B, there follows 8 ... Kt—B 6 *ch*.

5	Kt—B 5 *ch*	K—R 1
6	Kt—R 4	P × P
7	B × P	B × B
8	Q × B	P—Q 6

Now the diagonal aiming at White's K B 2 is open; Black's counter-attack has started.

9	K—R 1	R—B 7

The other Rook gets into play. A Rook on the 7th is always dangerous. There is nothing much left of White's original attack.

10	R—K 3	R (B 1) × P
11	Kt—Kt 2	P—Q 7
12	R—K Kt 1	R—Q B 8
13	Q—K 7	R × R *ch*
14	K × R	P—Q 8 (Q) *ch*

and Black mates in a few moves.

During the battle of the Marne, Foch wrote, "My front is broken, my right wing is retreating, my left wing is in flight, I counter-attack."

Diag. 63 presents us with a magnificent example of a counter-attack which has practically become a necessity, since a passive defence would almost certainly have led to disaster. White's Kt at Q 4 is pinned, nor can his Queen leave the Q file to relieve the pin as then the Kt would be lost. As Black also threatens to win this Kt by ... Kt—B 4; White is unable to make the necessary

DIAGRAM 63

White: Lasker; *Black:* Janowski
Match, 1910

preparations for castling. Thus the King must remain
in the centre: most players would lose heart in such
circumstances. But with admirable calm White extri-
cates himself from this parlous situation and, aided by
some timid moves by his adversary, even succeeds in
winning the game brilliantly.

White's chief weakness is his King's exposed position
in the centre, therefore he must at all costs make castling
possible. Next he must attend to his Kt at Q 4: here
counter-threats will come into play.

    1   P—Q Kt 4   Q—K 4

It is strange that Janowski, a most enterprising player,
should have missed the continuation: 1 ... B × P; 2
P × B, Q × P; 3 R—B 1, Kt—B 4; or, better still, the
more subtle : 1 ... Kt × P; 2 P × Kt, B × P; 3 R × Q,
B × Kt *ch*; 4 K—K 2, (4 B—Q 2, R × Kt); B × R,
etc.

    2   Kt (B 3)—Kt 5

A most ingenious defence of the Kt at Q 4. He

could have guarded this piece by 2 Kt (B 3)—K 2, but his B would have been shut in and all hope of castling would have vanished. But now he has the chance of an attack. For instance, against 2 ... P—R 3; he can play the Queen to B 1, pinning Black's Q Kt with a strong attack, e.g.: 3 Q—B 1, P × Kt; 4 Kt × Kt, P × Kt; 5 Q × P *ch*, Q—B 2; 6 Q—R 6 *ch*, etc. Still stronger would be: 3 Kt × Kt, R × Q *ch*; 4 R × R, and it is difficult for Black to defend himself against White's multiple threats. The position is full of potential combinations.

| 2 ... | Kt—B 4 |

The King cannot move away as 3 Kt × Kt *ch*, would make everything safe.

| 3 R—B 1 |

By pinning Black's Q Kt, White safeguards his own. He gives up a pawn to relieve the pressure.

| 3 ... | Kt × B |

To accept the offer is doubtful policy. He could have continued the attack by 3 ... B—K 2.

| 4 P × Kt | Q × P *ch* |
| 5 B—K 2 | B—K 2 |

Well played ! The Q R is now guarded and another piece comes into play. Had he played 5 ... B—Kt 6; as has been suggested, the dangers of his position would have stood out clearly after 6 Kt × P *ch*, K—B 2 (6 ... K—Kt 1; 7 Kt (Q 4) × Kt *ch*); 7 Kt (Q 4)—Kt 5 *ch*, K—Kt 3 (7 ... K—Kt 1; 8 Q × R *ch*, with 9 R—B 8 *mate*); 8 R × Kt *ch*, P × R; 9 Q × R *ch*, and wins.

| 6 R—B 3 |

If the Q moves White can castle, maintaining his attack against the black King. Should black meekly forgo his advantage or continue the attack ? In the latter case,

Black again would have an interesting combination, as follows: 6 ... Q × R *ch*; 7 Kt × Q, Kt × Kt; with many prospective chances. But once more he cannot summon up the necessary pluck.

| 6 | ... | B—R 5 *ch* |
| 7 | P—Kt 3 | Q—K 5 |

Had Black played ... B—K 2; on his third move, his Queen would still be at K 4, and he could have continued with ... B × P *ch*; demolishing White's K side.

| 8 | Castles | B—B 3 |
| 9 | R × B | |

White, on the contrary, counter-attacks with vigour. He eliminates a piece which attacks his Knight, and as Black's K R is out of play, he has an extra piece to take part in the attack.

| 9 | ... | P × R |
| 10 | B—B 3 | Q—K 4 |

Three white pieces are now attacking the Knight, which is guarded only once.

11	Kt × P *ch*	K—B 2
12	Kt (R 7) × Kt	P × Kt
13	R × P *ch*	K—Kt 1
14	R—Kt 6 *ch*	K—B 1
15	Q—B 1 *ch*	K—Q 2
16	Kt × B	and White won in a few moves.

A player who is at a positional disadvantage can have recourse to an attack in order to redress the balance, even when his opponent is not conducting an attack, but is endeavouring to crush him by simple positional manœuvres. This cannot be termed a counter-attack, since there is no attack. Nevertheless, an illustration of such a case is appropriate here.

White's advantage in the position shown in Diag. 64

DIAGRAM 64

White: Euwe; *Black:* Alekhine
Match, 1935

is obvious. Black's position shows a number of weak-nesses, and his pieces are badly placed. White even threatens to launch a K side attack by 1 P—K Kt 4, or, alternatively, he could start an action on the other wing, aiming at the weak squares at Q B 6, Q 6, and K 6. Black therefore gives him the opportunity of a com-bination which, however, eliminates White's attacking Bishop.

1	Kt × P	B × B
2	Kt × Q P	Q—Kt 1
3	Kt × P	B—B 3
4	Kt—Q 2	

Black now has won a piece for three united pawns, of which two are passed pawns in the centre—not a particularly favourable exchange. But in giving his adversary this opportunity, Black had something else in view, as the sequel shows.

    4   ...   P—K Kt 4
Having eliminated the hostile Bishop and holding the

long diagonal with his own, he now begins a K side attack
which counteracts the advance of the pawns in the centre.

5	P—K 4	P × P
6	P × P	B—Q 5

Evidently he cannot allow his Bishop to be shut in.

7	P—K 5	Q—K 1
8	P—K 6	R—K Kt 1

Combining already ! If 9 P × Kt, Q—K 7; wins the
Kt and White's disrupted pawns are powerless.

9	Kt—B 3	Q—Kt 3

Black probably visualised this combination when playing his first move. He clearly has obtained a very strong
attacking position, and White will need no little ingenuity
in order to steer clear of disaster.

10	R—K Kt 1

Such are the desperate means to which White must
have recourse to save the game. He gives up the
exchange for the sake of eliminating the well-posted
black Bishop. He can then hope to regain the initiative
by occupying the long black diagonal with his Queen,
and with a Rook on the K Kt file.

10	...	B × R
11	R × B	

Hypnotised by the long diagonal, Black played here
11 ... Q—B 3; and finally lost the game. He probably
could have drawn by 11 ... Q—B 4; closing the diagonal
with 12 ... Kt—B 3; or, if 12 P × Kt, R × R *ch*; with
perpetual check.

It remains to be said that, when launching an attack
from an inferior position, one does not necessarily play
all out for a win; a draw is a very satisfactory result. We
could add that, if such an attack leads to complications

in which the opponent might lose his way, it is preferable to a slow and certain loss.

It is a difficult task to combine a passive defence with a future attack, but, at times, this policy leads to surprising results. In order to elaborate such a system of defence, in which a prospective attack plays an important part, it is essential not only to grasp the salient points of the hostile attack, but also to foresee, at least on broad lines, the means of defence and the prospects of the counter-attack.

In Diag. 65 White has already initiated an assault on

DIAGRAM 65

White: Colle; *Black:* Znosko-Borovsky
Nice, 1930

the hostile K side, although the opening stage has barely been concluded. Black must take measures against the attack, and, if possible, repel it. His first move is:

　　1 ...　　　　　　　　R—B 2

With the idea of a passive defence of the Q B, and of placing the K Kt at K 5 after ... Q—R 1; thus closing the diagonal of the dangerous white K B. Incidentally,

this plan is intended to lead to a counter-attack on the
K side, at some unspecified future time, by means of
... P—B 4; and, if opportune, the advance of the
other K side pawns. Before the pawns on the attacked
flank can advance safely, a Rook must be posted behind
them. We have already seen a Rook participate in the
defence of the K side by taking up a position on the
second rank; in the present instance the idea of a prospective counter-attack is allied to this defensive scheme.

2	P—Kt 5	B × Kt
3	B P × B	Kt—K 5

As the K Kt P is no longer protected, this move can
be made without losing a pawn.

4	P—K R 4	P—B 4

With two white pieces out of play Black initiates his
counter-attack. At the moment he defends his Knight,
but already offers a pawn in sacrifice.

5	K P × P *e.p.*

He could have gained a pawn by 5 Kt P × P *e.p.*,
Kt P × P; 6 Q—Kt 4 *ch*, but Black's attack on the
K R and K Kt files would be too strong.

5	...	Kt P × P
6	P—Kt 6	

White is pressing on the attack rather than dis-
continuing it. Better would be 6 Kt × Kt.

6	...	P—B 4
7	B × Kt	

After 7 P × P *ch*, K—R 1; Black immediately occupies
the open files.

7	...	Q P × B
8	Q—Kt 3	R—K B 3

It would be simpler to play 8 ... Kt—B 3; in order
to bring the Q R into play more speedily.

9	P—R 5	P × Kt P
10	R—B 2	Kt—B 1
11	Kt—B 4	P × Q P
12	Kt—K 5	P × B P
13	P × B P	R—K R 2

At last, after 12 moves, Black's idea triumphs. With the entry of the Q R into the game on the K side, where White was attacking, the tide has turned and Black wrests the initiative from his adversary.

14	B—R 3	P × P

And finally Black won. It must not be thought that Black, in making his first move, foresaw the whole of the subsequent development; the fact of merely conceiving the idea enabled him to find the correct move on which his subsequent play was based.

At times, instead of a long and complicated counter-attack, a short and simple combination suffices to save the game, and if it is a case of a tactical opportunity and not a simple blunder on the part of the attacker, such a game may culminate in a brilliant finish. But as a general rule one can observe a certain degree of inattention on the part of the aggressor who, immersed in his own strategic plans and combinations, pays insufficient heed to his opponent's intentions.

In Diag. 66 White conducts what appears to be a winning attack. Probably he would have caused his opponent the most serious difficulties with 1 Kt—Q 6. Instead of that he continued in straightforward and humdrum fashion:

1	Kt—Kt 5	

This short-sighted move affords Black a tactical opportunity of which he is not slow to avail himself.

1	...	P—B 3

DIAGRAM 66

White: Landau; *Black:* Reshevsky
Kemeri, 1937

Although compulsory, this move gives Black unexpected chances; by opening the K B file, he threatens
White's K B P, and the power of the two Bishops becomes
devastating.

    2 P × P

The sacrifice of a Bishop by 2 B × P, etc., leads to
nothing, as can easily be ascertained.

    2 ...   B × P *ch*

It is possible that White had not foreseen this sacrifice
and that he only reckoned with the simple recapture
2 ... R × P.

    3 K × B   Q × P *ch*

As a result of his sacrifice Black can now recapture
with the Queen, threatening mate. White's next move
is therefore compulsory and his short-lived onslaught is
at an end.

    4 Kt—B 3   B × Kt
    5 P × B   Q × P *ch*
    6 K—Kt 1   R—B 5

The attack is now definitely in Black's hands, and, as is often the case with counter-attacks, it is immediately successful, the opponent's position being weakened. Black now threatens mate, and there is no defence.

7	Q × R	Kt × Q
8	B—B 1	R—B 4

and Black won easily.

(c) Exchanges

We have seen that the player who has the advantage often wishes to bring about an end game, because there his advantage will be of greater comparative value. Similarly there are cases where the weaker party will be actuated by the same desire when his disadvantage is likely to be less decisive in the end game. A seemingly lost game can often be saved in that way. The whole point of the matter is to be able to decide which type of end game would be the most advantageous and to know how to bring it about.

In Diag. 67 Black has a very bad game; he is losing

DIAGRAM 67

White: Schlechter; *Black:* Lasker
Match, 1911

a pawn whilst White has two united pawns on the K side; his pieces are so well placed that he can almost threaten mate. The end seems inevitable. How can such a position as Black's be saved?

1	R—B 7 *ch*	K—B 3

The King must avoid the first rank because of 2 R—B 8 *ch* or Kt—Kt 6 *ch*.

2	Kt—Q 5 *ch*	K—Kt 4

If 2 ... K—K 3; 3 P—B 4 (threatening mate), R—K 1; 4 R—K R 7, and wins.

3	P—R 4 *ch*	K—R 3
4	Kt—K 7	

The moment has arrived when Black must decide which course to pursue. He has three isolated pawns, of which one is attacked and another will be threatened (Q 3) on the next move. He cannot protect both and he must decide which one he is going to abandon and at what precise moment. The problem is not difficult but most instructive; it is fairly obvious that he cannot afford to let his K B P go as White would then have two united passed pawns. In other words, he must maintain this pawn at any cost.

4	...	R—K B 1
5	R—Q 1	

Another pawn is attacked and this one cannot be defended. Black seeks to reach an end game in which he is most likely to hold his own, namely, a R and P ending after exchanging the Knights.

5	...	R—B 2
6	R × P *ch*	K—R 2
7	R—K 6	Kt—Kt 3
8	R × Kt	R × Kt
9	R (Kt 6)—Q B 6	R × R

| 10 | R × R *ch* | K—Kt 3 |
| 11 | R—B 6 *ch* | K—B 2 |

This is exactly the ending which Black desired. But what shall we say when we see him deliberately giving up a second pawn in order to secure a draw ?

12	K—B 3	R—K 5
13	R—B 5	K—B 3
14	R × P	

And this ending leads to a forced draw ! Thanks to his grasp of the essentials of the position, Black has succeeded in holding his K B P and his position as well.

In Diag. 68 Black's position is manifestly inferior : not only is his Bishop pinned, but he is in consequence threatened with the loss of a pawn. At the same time his Q side pawns are weakened to such an extent that they will be very difficult to defend and the loss of another pawn is almost a foregone conclusion. Castling would be no remedy, as he would immediately lose a

DIAGRAM 68

White: Maróczy; *Black:* Tarrasch
San Sebastian, 1911

pawn in the centre after an exchange of minor pieces
and would still labour under his disability on the Q side,
leading to further loss.   His plan of defence develops as
follows: he will protect his B as much as possible and
use the time White will spend in attacking it on
improving his pawn position, finally letting the least
important pawn go.

	1 ...	K—K 2
	2 R—K 5	

Attacking the Q B P with a threat of doubling his Rooks.
2 P—K B 4, contains no immediate threat, because after
2 ... P—Kt 3; 3 P—Kt 4, the threat of 4 P—B 5 is not
dangerous, e.g., 4 ... P×P; 5 P×P, R—K Kt 1;
threatening the Knight which is now pinned.

2	...	Q R—Q B 1
3	Q R—K 1	R—B 3
4	P—K B 4	P—Kt 3
5	P—Kt 4	

The decisive moment !   White threatens both P—
B 5, and Kt—K 4, attacking either the B or the Q B P.
If Black plays ... K R—Q B 1; both his Rooks will be
tied to the defence of the pawns.

	5 ...	P—B 5

Countering White's intentions and threatening to
advance still further.

	6 P—R 4	

Preparing the advance of the K B P, but K—B 2,
would have been better.

6	...	P—R 3
7	Kt × B	R × Kt
8	R × R ch	P × R
9	P—B 5	P × P
10	P × P	K—B 3

11   R × P *ch*   K × P
12   R × Q R P

White has won a pawn, but in consequence of Black's skilful manœuvring, it is only a R P. White has only four pawns left, of which the K R P is threatened by the well-posted King; in addition, Black's two Q side pawns are very strong and his Rook is admirably posted. The game ended in a draw.

(d)   Bringing about an End Game

In a way, the transition into the end game is an example of simplification by exchanges. The attacker exchanges such of his pieces as do not contribute to his superiority against the well-developed pieces of his opponent. The defender acts in a similar manner, following the precept that, wherever possible, it is of advantage for him to exchange his passive pieces for his opponent's more active pieces. There are numerous examples, but we shall only give one, a well-known one from the openings. It is a variation of the Queen's Gambit Declined, Orthodox Defence, in which, by a subtle

DIAGRAM 69

manœuvre, Black brings about the exchange of three of his pieces, and, as White's attack has now lost much of its sting, Black should emerge unscathed, after which his prospects for the end game, with three pawns against two on the Q side, will be favourable.

1 ... P × P; 2 B × P, Kt—Q 4; 3 B × B, Q × B; 4 Castles, Kt × Kt; 5 R × Kt, P—K 4; 6 Kt × P, Kt × Kt; 7 P × Kt, Q × Kt; etc.

IV. EVEN POSITIONS

1. COMBINATION OF THE ELEMENTS

We now come to the most important as well as the
most difficult part of our studies—even positions. They
are important because they will occur every time we
play chess, the initial position being even and remaining
so after every correctly played opening; and difficult
because the objective is less clear than in any other part
of the game. It is easy to attack when we know what
we seek to achieve, nor is it difficult to decide on a
defence when we know where our weakness lies. But
in a position of equality players are often at a loss what
to do, and what to seek, and handicapped, moreover, by a
well-grounded fear that an unconsidered move or a lack
of understanding of the position may give the opponent
an advantage leading to a win.

It must not be thought that in such positions there is
equality in every respect. There may have been a loss
in one element, a gain in another, which may balance
each other and produce equality in the position as a
whole.

Take, for instance, the position in Diag. 70. The
positions are entirely dissimilar; each has its own chances,
its own difficulties. White, for instance, cannot castle
on the K side, nor can he develop his Bishop without
losing a pawn. On the other hand, Black has an isolated
as well as a doubled pawn, his Bishop is shut in, and it
will not be easy for him to castle.

1   Castles

A risky move seeking, at the cost of a pawn, to take

DIAGRAM 70

White: Lasker; *Black:* Marshall
Match, 1907

advantage of the position of Black's King in the centre
by initiating a direct attack.

     1   ...   Q × R P

We see that an equal position does not necessarily lead
to slow and uninteresting play.

     2   P—Q 5   P × P
     3   B—Kt 5   K—B 1
     4   B × Kt   P × B
     5   Q × K B P

Threatening both Kt—Kt 5, and K R—K 1, whilst the
Queen maintains the protection of the weak Q Kt P.

     5   ...   Q—R 8 *ch*
     6   K—Q 2   Q—R 4 *ch*
     7   P—B 3   R—Kt 1

Because the Q Kt P is now left unguarded. If 8 R—
Q Kt 1, P—Q 5; and the Black Queen defends her
K Kt 4; and if then 9 Q × Q P, B—B 4.

8	Kt—Kt 5	R × P *ch*
9	K—K 1	R × Kt

The only defence against Q × P *mate*. Now if White captures the R, Black threatens ... B—R 3; and ... Q × P *ch*.

10	Q—Q 8 *ch*	K—Kt 2
11	Q × R *ch*	K—B 1

And this lively game ended in a draw.

Even positions can show still greater discrepancies in various elements than those illustrated in the preceding example. Each side may be conducting an attack on opposite wings. In such cases great caution is necessary, as always when there is only a small advantage. But when an attack is launched where the attacker has a marked advantage on one side and a disadvantage on the other (where the opponent is attacking), it is often essential to throw in all one's resources, in order to be first in reaching the objective.

This state of affairs obtains in the position shown in Diag. 71. The sequel is an extraordinary example of chess of the highest class.

A complete analysis from the point of view of our three elements would show that the position is one of equality, the difference being that White is more active and has, in particular, a K side attack, whilst Black has threats on the Q side. White's attack is the more dangerous inasmuch as it can lead to a mate, but there is no weakness in Black's camp and his plan will be to hold White's attack and to obtain a preponderance on the Q side with the ultimate object of obtaining an advanced passed pawn and queening it.

This result is not an unlikely one as Black's pieces are as well posted as White's, although they are less active.

DIAGRAM 71

White: Pillsbury; *Black:* Tarrasch
Hastings, 1895

But his Rooks are admirably placed and able to support the advance of the pawns. Black has a pawn-majority on the Q side, which is of considerable importance, especially in view of the fact that White's extra pawn on the K side (his K P) is backward and plays, and always will play, a secondary rôle.

Thus White's only hope is centred in his attack, whilst Black has every incentive to bring about an end game. His first concern will be to stand up against the storm which presently will break. That the situation is extremely critical can be seen from the following variation: let Black play 1 ... Kt—K 3; and he loses forthwith, as follows: 2 B × Kt, B × B; 3 B × P *ch*, K × B; 4 Q—R 5 *ch*, K—Kt 1; 5 Q × P *ch*, followed by 6 Q × Q B. The defence clearly calls for the utmost caution. But Black, unless he makes a careless move, is for the moment sufficiently well protected, while White, in order to succeed with his attack, must bring up another piece.

The question is which ? Either the Q Kt or the K R
by opening the K Kt file by P—K Kt 4, which is a
lengthy and risky manœuvre. In the meantime Black
will advance his Q side pawns, but without haste, as he
might obtain a passed but isolated pawn which could
easily be stopped. The only pieces available for the
support of the pawn-advance are the Rooks, the other
pieces being required for the defence of the King's field,
although it may become possible for one or the other,
especially the Queen, to combine both tasks—the defence
of the King's field and the support of the Q side pawns.
Thus Black's threat also demands a great deal of time,
for which reason the positions may be said to be even.

1	Kt—K 2	Kt—K 5

Every exchange is in Black's favour, as thereby the
defence becomes easier, the attacking forces are dim-
inished in numbers and the end game is so much nearer.
The text move, at one stroke, deals with his adversary's
two Bishops, as the exchange is forced because of the
threatened advance of Black's K B P to B 3.

2	B × B	R × B
3	B × Kt	P × B
4	Q—Kt 3	

The first skirmish is over, and we can take stock of
the new situation. White has obtained a passed pawn
and has weakened Black's Q side pawns. He now
threatens P—B 5, followed by Kt—B 4, bringing up the
additional piece which was needed for the attack. His
K P is strengthened by the fact that the K file is now
closed, and thus no attack is to be feared at the moment.
What has Black achieved ? He has eliminated White's
two Bishops and freed his Q 4. From this point either
his Q or his B can assume the twofold task which we

have mentioned, namely, defence of his King's field and support of his Q side pawns. Again the positions are more or less balanced. The interesting part of this game lies precisely in the fact that, up to the end, it is played by both sides with the greatest mastery, so that any advantage gained by either player is immediately neutralised by a corresponding gain by his rival. This is why we give a more complete analysis of this important contest. Considerations of space preclude our treating other games in the same way, but the reader can do this for himself.

What are now White's actual threats ? He can advance the K B P and attack Black's isolated K P. To this end he will need 7 moves (P—B 5, Q—R 4, R—B 1, R—B 4, Kt—Kt 4, Kt—B 2, Kt—Kt 3 or Kt—B 3) and Black, in order to defend the pawn, needs but 5 moves (P—B 3, B—Q 4, Q—Q 2, Q—B 3, Q R—K 1); he has therefore ample time, which is the justification for his previous exchanges. He can utilise his extra *tempi* in advancing his Q side pawns. In any event he will have to make a supplementary defensive move, for after Kt—Kt 4, White threatens Kt × P *ch*, or Kt—R 6 *ch*, which forces ... K—R 1. The claims of the defence are paramount for Black and moves on the Q side can only be entertained by him as long as his K side is secure.

4	...	P—B 3
5	Kt—Kt 4	K—R 1
6	P—B 5	Q—Q 2
7	R—B 1	R—Q 1
8	R—B 4	Q—Q 3
9	Q—R 4	Q R—K 1
10	Kt—B 3	B—Q 4
11	Kt—B 2	Q—B 3

A fresh series of moves, embodying the next manœuvre, is thus completed, and again a position of stable equilibrium has resulted. We must, however, record the fact that Black, with some moves to spare, has marked time, and has accomplished nothing with his Q side pawns; at the moment this wavering has no serious consequences, but when the crisis arrives it may be that one single move may save or win the game. All Black's pieces are now·available for the defence and nothing stands in the way of the beginning of his advance on the Q side. His plan is clear: ... P—Kt 5; and, after White's Q Kt has departed, ... Q—R 5; attacking the Q R P, with the object of either weakening White's pawn formation or of causing him to withdraw some of his pieces from the attack. Black has every justification for commencing his advance; he has made 18 useful moves against 12 by White, or, in other words, he is 6 moves ahead. It is difficult to see how White, who has also made only good moves, can have lost so much time ! It is a curious and frequently observed fact that, in order to obtain an attacking position, it is often necessary to sacrifice time, and in the present game we shall have occasion to note that Black himself will be in the same predicament as soon as he starts to execute his threats on the Q side.

White's next problem is to bring up another piece for the attack, this time the Q R after P—K Kt 4, which move can be made with safety now that Black's K P intercepts the line of his Bishop.

12	R—B 1	P—Kt 5
13	Kt—K 2	Q—R 5

An immediate advance by the Q B P would be of little use, e.g. : 13 ... P—B 6; 14 P×P, P×P; 15 Kt—Q 1, P—B 7; 16 K Kt—B 3, B—B 5; 17 P—Q 5,

B × Q P; 18 R—B 1, and the Q B P falls. But now
White is facing a serious problem—how to protect his
Q R P. If 14 Kt—B 1, then 14 ... Q—B 7; attacking
the Q Kt P, followed by ... Q—Q 6; attacking the K P.
The solution is to combine attack and defence, and this
White does in a manner as well-calculated as it is
attractive.

> 14 Kt—Kt 4

Threatening Kt × P. As soon as a black piece has been
withdrawn from the defence, its absence is felt.

> 14 ...   Kt—Q 2

It is a pity to have to displace this Knight which was so
well placed for the defence of the K R P, and the squares
at Black's K 3 and K Kt 3. But unless Black resigns
himself to a purely defensive game and forgoes any
attempt to win, he has to take a certain amount of risk.

> 15 R (B 4)—B 2

A subtle defence of the Q R P. The Rook makes room
for a Knight and if 15 ... Q × P; then 16 Kt—B 4,
(threatening Kt—Kt 6 ch), B—B 2; 17 Kt—Kt 6 ch,
B × Kt; 18 P × B, P—R 3; 19 Kt × R P, winning easily.
Again the withdrawal of a piece from its defensive
position has conjured up all sorts of difficulties—even
threats of mate. It is clear that White's Q R P cannot,
as yet, be captured.

> 15 ...   K—Kt 1
> 16 Kt—B 1

And now the square Q B 2 is guarded as well as the
Q R P.

> 16 ...   P—B 6
> 17 P—Q Kt 3   Q—B 3

If we now count the moves, we shall see that Black
has the same number, 18, as before to his credit, whilst

White has 16 instead of 12; he has gained 4 moves, confirming what we said before.

The game is now nearing its end; threats are less numerous but more intense. White has thrown the whole of his forces into the attack except the Q Kt, which is attending to the defence—splendid strategy. All of Black's pieces are co-operating in the defence. But if he wishes to succeed with his own attack he will have to detail at least one piece for that purpose. What is his plan of attack in the present circumstances ? The only possible one is to advance the R P and exchange it for the Q Kt P; then he will occupy the Q R file with a Rook and attack the Q Kt P with R and B. It is possible to calculate exactly the number of moves required in the process. The number is 4 moves; on the 5th move the Q Kt P will be attacked twice. Now what of White ? Again there is only one possible plan: the opening of the K Kt file. This also will require 4 moves, but on the 4th move the K B P will be already under attack. Had Black not lost one or two moves in his earlier manœuvres his threat would be the first to mature.

18	P—K R 3	P—Q R 4
19	Kt—R 2	P—R 5
20	P—Kt 4	

Now Black must decide between two courses: he must either ruthlessly continue the advance on the Q side or take some defensive measures to stop White's advance on the K side. This he could achieve by 20 ... P—R 3; upon which White would have to play 21 Q—Kt 3 (preparing for P—R 4), and Black would have time to defend himself by 21 ... Kt—B 1; 22 P—R 4, Kt—R 2; 23 P—Kt 5, K R P × P; 24 Kt—Kt 4, P × R P; 25 Q × P, Kt—Kt 4; threatening 26 ... Kt—B 6 ch. If

25 R—R 2, then 25 ... K—B 1; leaving it to the Bishop
to guard Black's K Kt 1. Thus even against a passive
defence White would not find it easy to utilise the open·
file and bring the missing piece—the Rook—into the
attack.   But Black prefers to attack himself, in the belief
that he will reach his objective ahead of his adversary.

| 20 | ... | P × P |
| 21 | P × P | R—R 1 |

DIAGRAM 72

22   P—Kt 5

Let us examine the respective threats. If Black exchanges pawns, then 23 Q × Kt P (threatening P—B 6),
Q—B 3; 24 Q—Kt 3, threatening Kt—Kt 4.   There is
no defence against P—B 6, and Kt—K 5.   If instead
of 23 ... Q—B 3; Black plays 23 ... Kt—B 3; then
again 24 Kt—Kt 4, follows, threatening both Kt—
K 5, and R—K Kt 2 (the Knight cannot be taken because
of Q × R).   Therefore Black cannot himself take the
pawn, but must leave it to White to effect the exchange.
He can thus get in a move in furtherance of his own
attack.

22 ...   R—R 6
23 Kt—Kt 4

White would gain nothing by capturing the K B P
at once, as Black would recapture with the pawn or even
the Queen and after Q—Kt 3, he would play ... P—R 4;
preventing Kt—Kt 4. Hence White plays the text-
move, threatening P × P, and giving up the Q Kt P.
We have now reached the turning point in the battle.
Both players had anticipated this position many moves
ahead and had analysed it thoroughly.

If we now count the moves we find that Black has 17
moves against 19 by White. Against this deficit of 2
moves he can win a pawn. But this pawn is on the Q
side and can only be of value if White's attack should
fail. But White is on the point of opening the K Kt
file and of bringing into play the additional piece which
is required: his object is then achieved. The climax of
the game is at hand, the issue hangs by a thread. The
next few moves will decide the battle and confirm or
refute the players' calculations.

Black cannot take the K Kt P (23 ... P × P; 24 Q × P,
Kt—B 3; 25 R—K Kt 2, with a winning attack) and he
must therefore take the Q Kt P, the object of his attack,
and hope for the best. After 23 ... B × P; White cannot
play 24 Kt × B, R × Kt; because of ... R—Kt 7; which
would nullify the effect of White's Rook at K Kt 2. He
therefore plays his Rook to K Kt 2 first, forcing the
black King to move.

23 ...   B × P
24 R—K Kt 2   K—R 1
25 P × P   P × P

If 25 ... Kt × P; 26 Kt—K 5, threatening 27 Kt—
Kt 6 *ch.*

26	Kt × B	R × Kt
27	Kt—R 6	

With a terrible mating threat by R—Kt 8. If 27 ...
R—K 1; 28 Kt—B 7, *mate*.   Two white squares are
defenceless because the Bishop has gone. The extra
piece which White has at last succeeded in bringing into
the attack decides the game. The black King, denuded
of pieces, is defenceless against the powerful threats.

Thus White's strategy has triumphed.

There is one point, however, to which we wish to
draw the reader's attention. The game is lost because
Black lacks the help of his Bishop. If he had captured
the Q Kt P with his Rook, giving up the exchange, he
would have preserved his Bishop, which was so essential
for the defence, and the two united passed pawns, supported by the Bishop, would have been more than a
match for a Rook. Black had this tactical opportunity
and failed to take it. Either he did not see it, or he
underestimated the dangers of the situation, or he
lacked the pluck to make this sacrifice. White, on the
other hand, did not hesitate to sacrifice a whole Kt.
Black did not lose because of a faulty conception; his
tactical failure in its execution was his downfall.

27	...	R—Kt 2
28	R × R	K × R
29	Q—Kt 3 *ch*	K × Kt
30	K—R 1	

The plausible 30 R—B 4, would be bad because of
checks by Black's Rook on its 7th and 8th ranks.

30	...	Q—Q 4
31	R—K Kt 1	Q × B P
32	Q—R 4 *ch*	Q—R 4
33	Q—B 4 *ch*	Q—Kt 4

34	R × Q	P × R
35	Q—Q 6 *ch*	K—R 4
36	Q × Kt and wins owing to the threat of	

Q × P *mate*.

Nothing could be more instructive than the analysis of such a game.

2.   Positions Without Distinctive Features

Equal positions which show no particular characteristics are the most difficult to treat. Such positions occur most frequently when the opening stage has been passed, and the examples we shall give could serve equally well as illustrations of the period of transition between the opening and the middle game; but the same sort of thing can equally well arise in the middle game proper.

If there is no weakness, with the forces on either side equally well developed and "nothing to get hold of," a puzzling problem immediately arises as to what to do. Still greater is the difficulty where the positions are almost identical; it seems that there is nothing one can do but to wait and see what the opponent is going to do, and watch whether he makes a weak move. But, with the exception of entirely symmetrical positions, it is rare indeed for a position to show no distinctive feature at all. It may not be pronounced, it may be subtle and difficult to discover, but it is nearly always there and requires careful consideration. In the case of symmetrical positions, it is well known that it is not practicable for one player to copy his opponent's moves *ad infinitum*; there must come a time, even in such cases, when some difference occurs which may give rise to a plan, be it ever so cautious and slow.

The positions in Diag. 73 are almost symmetrical, the only difference being that White's K B is at B 2, and Black's at Kt 3.   Is this sufficient to serve as a basis for

DIAGRAM 73

White: Riga; *Black:* Berlin
A correspondence game, 1905

a plan of campaign ?   White would only need to play his Bishop to Kt 3 or Black to move his own to B 2 to restore the symmetry; and that is what not a few players, devotees of the draw, would do.   But if the object is to try to take advantage of the respective positions of the Bishops, there would arise many interesting, and possibly conclusive, considerations.   It seems that Black's K B is the better placed; it controls an open diagonal, and if White plays the obvious P—Q 4, that pawn would be in the line of the Bishop.   On the other hand, White's K B is blocked by his own centre pawns.   In analysing the position more closely, certain points will come to

our notice which will alter our first impression. First
of all, White, in playing P—Q 4, closes the black
Bishop's diagonal, which then cannot be reopened, whilst
Black cannot play the equally natural move ... P—Q 4;
because on the one hand his K P is insufficiently protected, and on the other, White could open the diagonal
for his own K B by exchanging pawns. A further
distinction is that Black's K B is directed against White's
K B P which is sufficiently guarded, whereas White's
K B aims at the K R P, always susceptible to a sudden
attack.   The white Bishop's diagonal must not therefore
be opened, and such obvious moves as ... P—Q 4;
... P—K B 4; and ... Kt—B 5; cannot be commended.
As against this, White can afford to make any moves
that would help a sound development as well as a
prospective attack. If we add that White has the
move, we can clearly perceive that he has whatever
advantage there is. He now has the choice of several
lines of play; after his first move P—Q 4, he can continue with B—Kt 5, threatening Kt—R 5, or with
Kt—B 5. In this case, if Black plays ... B × Kt; P × B,
the pawn at K B 5 remains under the protection of
the K B.

If Black, however, plays ... B—Kt 5; there is no
need for White to play P—K R 3. He can play Q—Q 3,
and allow his pawns to be doubled. Black could not
easily take advantage of it by playing ... Kt—B 5;
because after B × Kt, P × B; this pawn is unguarded.
Thus, the more closely we examine the position, the
more do we realise that White's K B at B 2 is more
effective than its counterpart at Kt 3.

All this tends to show that White's game is the more
aggressive and that Black should be content quietly to

complete his development, the most natural course being
... R—K 1; ... B—K 3; ... P—K R 3; ... Q—B 2;
... Q R—Q 1; and to counter White's prospective K
side attack by counter play in the centre. The alternative, re-establishing the symmetry by ... B—B 2; would
mean for him a disadvantage in time of two moves.

But Black, having deliberately placed his K B at Kt 3,
desires to take the utmost advantage of this, in his
opinion, favourable position, and initiates an attack. We
must not be surprised if it fails—it is but justice! The
sequel shows in an instructive manner the consequences
of an action which does not conform to the nature of the
position, and of a strategic plan based on an erroneous
assumption, or a wrong appreciation of the situation.

1	P—Q 4	B—Kt 5
2	Q—Q 3	Kt—R 4

A vain attempt to establish this Knight at K B 5.

3	Kt × Kt	B × Kt (R 4)
4	B—Kt 5	Q—B 2
5	Kt—Q 2	

Now Black's Q B, like his K B, is also out of play and
has no move. He persists in trying to assume the
initiative — when the defensive was his proper course —
with a view to bringing his Bishops back into the game,
as, e.g., by ... Kt—K 2; ... P—B 3; ... B—B 2; after
which the Kt could go back to Kt 3.

5	...	P—K R 3
6	B—K 3	Q R—K 1
7	P—B 3	

Defending the K P and threatening at the same time
to win the Q B. With no thought for his own safety,
Black maintains his attack. It may be noted that White

disregards the hostile K B and has all but opened its diagonal, directed against the white King.

7	...	P—Q 4
8	P—K Kt 4	K P × P
9	B P × P	P—Q B 4
10	Q—B 3	Kt—B 5
11	B × Kt	Q × B
12	P × B	B P × P
13	.Q—Q 3	

and Black's attack has melted away.

This example has shown us how a plan can be built up on a minute positional difference. The idea, however, was wrong and the attack collapsed. Let us examine another example in which the difference in the positions is equally insignificant. But here there is no misconception and the game develops slowly, as it should, where the position shows no pronounced characteristics.

In Diag. 74 the difference between the two camps lies in the position of the respective Bishops: White's Bishops

DIAGRAM 74

White: Rubinstein; *Black:* Duras
Carlsbad, 1911

are well developed and bear on the centre, whilst Black's Bishops stand passively on their original squares, capable, however, of initiating an action in the centre or on either flank. There is no question of an attack, but of slow and well-considered manœuvres. White's first object is clear: by playing P—Q 4, White prevents a similar answer by Black and fixes Black's Q P, a backward and isolated pawn, at his Q 3. Of course, White will not capture the K P, which would only round off the adverse position; nor does he intend leaving his own Q P at Q 4, threatened by Black after ... B—Kt 5. His real intention is the further advance P—Q 5.

Now Black's backward Q P will prevent any action by the black Rooks on the Q file, besides hindering the free circulation of the black pieces, by dividing Black's position in two.

In order to get his attack going White will have to break up the black Q side and take it in the flank with his Rooks and, especially, with his Kt and B. Black can answer with the well-known advance ... P—K B 4; though it weakens the K P. He also has the chance of attacking White's K B by the equally popular manœuvre B—K R 6, but that will imply play on the K side. And now the problem is: shall he undertake an action on the K side on the lines indicated, or shall he, on the contrary, take advantage of the weaknesses created by White's P—Q 4, and counter-attack on the Q side? In order to decide the respective value of these two plans of campaign it would almost be necessary to play two games to try them out; in the present instance Black decided on action on the K side; he failed and there is no merit in stating that he should have tried the other method.

    1   P—Q 4   B—Kt 5

| 2   P—Q 5 | Kt—K 2 |

In accordance with what has been said before, this
Knight should preferably have moved to Kt 1 and from
there to R 3 or Q 2 threatening B 4 or Kt 5 respectively.

| 3   Q—Q 3 | Q—Q 2 |
| 4   Kt—Q 2 | B—R 6 |

Thus White manœuvres his pieces towards the Q side
and Black brings his forces to the opposite wing. Later
on Black will find out that his pressure is not equal to
his adversary's, and will attempt to remedy the defect
by calling his forces back to the right place. By then it
will be too late; the time thus gained by White gives
him a manifest advantage.

5   P—R 4

The object of this move is to place his Knight at Q B 4,
where he will be unmolested. At the same time it
initiates the pawn advance on the Q side.

| 5   ... | B × B |
| 6   K × B | K R—Kt 1 |

At last Black gives a thought to the Queen's wing; he
tries to isolate and weaken the adverse pawn, a faulty
enterprise which runs counter to the principle: "Never
open a line where you are weakest." But Black's real
difficulty is his Knight's unhappy position. Moreover,
it cannot return to the Q side, nor could it find a good
square if it did get there.

| 7   Kt—B 4 | P—Q Kt 4 |
| 8   P × P | Q × P |

The position has become clearer. White is attacking the
Q R P and Q P and Black has designs on the Q Kt P.

9 R—R 3	Kt—Kt 3
10 K R—Q R 1	P—R 3
11 B—B 1	

From Kt 2 this Bishop could not participate in the action on the Q side. It makes its way to a square from where it attacks the adverse Q R P. The fall of this pawn is a foregone conclusion. It is defended by the Queen and two Rooks. But B—K 3, will deprive the defence of one of the Rooks. White, on the other hand, can attack it three times, whilst safeguarding his own Q Kt P by Kt—Q 2. Observe that the black Knight requires at least three moves (B 1, Q 2, Kt 1) to come to the rescue. So much time is not available. As we have said, faulty mobilisation can seldom be rectified.

11	...	R—Kt 2
12	B—K 3	P—B 3
13	P—B 3	

Well played ! He provides against the hostile threat of ... P—B 4; before embarking on his own schemes. If, for instance, 13 Q—B 1, P—B 4; 14 P—B 3, P×P; 15 P×P, R—K B 2; Black has a strong attack. After the move in the text, Black cannot yet play 13 ... P—B 4; and White has time to play the necessary Kt—Q 2.

13	...	Kt—K 2
14	Q—B 1	Kt—B 1
15	Kt—Q 2	

The desired position is now attained and Black's pawn is lost.

15	...	Q—Kt 5
16	Q—B 4	

White forces the exchange of Queens to prevent any hostile attack; he relies on his extra pawn to secure a win.

16	...	Q×Q
17	Kt×Q	Q R—Kt 1
18	Kt—Q 2	

Guarding the Q Kt P; the hostile pawn cannot be saved.

18   ...   R—Q B 2
19   R × P   R—B 7
20   R (R 6)—R 2   R × R
21   R × R and White won without difficulty.

Games are lost through big or small mistakes; the last two games, starting from even positions, were lost on account of erroneous strategic ideas. As strategic plans can be evolved only on the basis of a thorough analysis of the position, this analysis is absolutely essential in positions which are lacking in definite character. Only a minute analysis can help to discover those small details, at first sight insignificant, which can serve as a starting point for an elaborate plan of campaign.

3. Upsetting the Balance

Of paramount importance in even positions is the moment when the balance is about to be disturbed. This does not necessarily happen in consequence of an attack; simple and slow manœuvring inevitably leads to it. It is an anxious moment, for it means taking a path from which there is no turning back; nor can one be quite sure where it is going to lead. But the Russians have a proverb which says: "For fear of the wolves one might never go into the forest": chess players must take certain risks or give up playing chess. Cannot the very first move be said to disturb the balance of the position ?

The position in Diag. 75 is perfectly even and is near the end game stage. Even though White has an extra move and a pawn in the centre, it amounts to little in this position. Even Black's doubled pawns do not represent a real weakness, as White lacks the necessary minor

DIAGRAM 75

White: Schlechter; *Black:* Lasker
Match, 1911

pieces to take advantage of the fact, and these pawns are able to hold quite easily the opposing three pawns. Each side has a majority of four pawns to three on opposite wings, but as the K P counterbalances the Q P this again amounts to nothing. The positions must undoubtedly be pronounced even, and in any event White has nothing to fear. An agreed draw would be justified. But if the game is to be continued, the line of play on either side is fairly obvious. If White wishes to turn his majority on the K side to account, he will have to divert Black's Q P, which means he must advance his own Q B P far forward, and this again will accentuate Black's majority on the Q side.

White therefore begins with manœuvres by which he seeks to weaken the adverse pawn formation.

1	Q—Kt 4	P—Q B 3
2	Q—R 3	P—R 3
3	Q—Kt 3	R—Q 1
4	P—Q B 4	

—in order to prevent the advance of the black Q P which has become weak.

4	...	R—Q 2
5	Q—Q 1	Q—K 4
6	Q—Kt 4	K—K 1
7	Q—K 2	K—Q 1
8	Q—Q 2	K—B 2

As White has failed to increase his advantage or to find a more or less direct line of action, Black now shows signs of activity; his King is no longer content to defend the weaker flank but, intending to assume the initiative, he wishes to support his strong Q side pawns. He evidently seeks to obtain a passed pawn there. The problem is how to achieve this without pawn exchanges with the prospect of remaining with an isolated pawn. Great caution is required; the pieces will have to work with the pawns in these operations.

9	P—R 3	R—K 2
10	P—Q Kt 4	P—Q Kt 4
11	P × P	R P × P

One object at least is achieved: a file is open on which stands a backward pawn. The King has relieved his pieces from the task of guarding the Q P, and the Queen and the Rook can strike out on a more enterprising line of play.

12	P—Kt 3	P—Kt 4
13	K—Kt 2	R—K 1
14	Q—Q 1	

White threatens both P—Q R 4 and Q—R 5. We see how much caution is required in a game of this type; any small advance creates weaknesses in one's own camp. Thus Black's threat to occupy the Q R file is held up and he must give some thought to his own safety.

14 ...   P—B 3

15 Q—Kt 3

White leaves the execution of his threats in abeyance.
It is true that, after 15 Q—R 5, Q—K 3; is a sufficient
defence, but he might at least have played 15 P—Q R 4.
He evidently prefers a passive defence, in order first to
ascertain his adversary's plans.

15 ...   Q—K 3

16 Q—Q 1

He probably thinks that an end game of Q and R affords
better chances of a draw than a simple R ending.

16 ...   R—K R 1

17 P—Kt 4

White's K side pawns are paralysed. Black's second
object is attained. He can now proceed with the third
stage of his plan: action against the Q side pawns.

17 ...   Q—B 5

Thus Black has acquired a dominating position, in
which his pieces are better placed than, and his pawns
superior to, his adversary's. White's Q R P in particular
is almost negligible. White clearly thinks so too, for
he tries to eliminate it by a sacrifice in order to regain
some measure of initiative. He should have thought of
that before the event.

18	P—Q R 4	Q × P
19	P × P	Q × P
20	R—Q Kt 3	Q—R 3
21	Q—Q 4	R—K 1
22	K—Kt 1	R—K 4

Black's advantage is clear-cut, and White's attack is not
a sufficient compensation for the loss of a pawn. Black
has demonstrated in a striking manner what can be made
of a drawn position. It must be added, however, that,

thanks to some tactical *finesse* by White and some tactical errors by his opponent, White ultimately won this game which might have been a masterpiece for Black.

In more complicated positions and with more pieces on the board, the balance can be upset more rapidly, more suddenly, and more decisively than in the preceding example. There may even be an attack, although, as we have seen, an attack can only be made in a superior position. It would be more correct to say that the attack should be made where one is strongest. We attack on the K side with, perhaps, an inferiority on the Q side. It is even a necessity, when to act otherwise means that the opponent is allowed full sway. Counter-attack as a means of defence is of the same type.

The position in Diag. 76 is still in the opening stages. It would be in order to proceed with a tranquil development. On the contrary, White commences without delay an aggressive action which forces his opponent to combine development with defence.

DIAGRAM 76

White: Spielmann; *Black:* Tartakower
Match, Vienna, 1913

| 1 | P—B 5 | P × P |
| 2 | Q × P | Kt—K 2 |

Black parries the check at his Q B 1 by developing a piece.

| 3 | Q—B 2 | Kt—Kt 3 |
| 4 | P—K R 4 | |

Such attacks without a well-defined object are to be deprecated. They only weaken the position without any appreciable compensation.

4	...	B—K 2
5	P—R 5	Kt—B 1
6	Kt—K 2	Kt—K 3

In consequence of White's attack this Knight is now on a far better square.

| 7 | P—B 3 | P—Q B 4 |

The K side being developed, Black commences an action on the Q side, which is far more justified than White's aggression on the opposite wing.

8	Kt—B 4	Kt × Kt
9	B × Kt	P × P
10	P × P	Kt—B 3
11	B—K 3	Castles K R

Black's development is completed, whilst White has not yet castled and one of his Knights is still on its original square.

| 12 | P—R 6 | P—Kt 3 |
| 13 | Kt—B 3 | P—B 3 |

Well played ! He now begins an action on the K side, where White's position is weakened in consequence of his premature attack.

| 14 | P × P | R × P |
| 15 | Q—Q 2 | B—Kt 5 |

Anticipating White's castling on the Q side—he has no choice—Black prepares an attack.

16	Castles	Kt—R 4
17	K—Kt 1	Kt—B 5

And Black has everything to hope for from his well-timed attack. White has upset the balance to his own disadvantage.

The destruction of the balance can also be caused by a simple combination which may call, in reply, for a counter-combination by the other side. Which goes to show that even positions do not of necessity imply dull and unimaginative play.

In Diag. 77 Black, after eliminating his doubled pawn, is in a favourable position with "two Bishops" and with both Rooks well developed. Against this White has the

DIAGRAM 77

White: Gunsberg; *Black:* Przepiórka
San Remo, 1911

outline of an attack, so that the games may be said to be even, with the odds slightly in favour of Black. It is not, therefore, surprising to see White embark upon a combination.

1	Q—Kt 4	P—Q R 4

	2	P×P	Q×P
	3	Kt×P	

This sacrifice brings a little life into a rather colourless position. The Knight cannot be taken as Black would then lose one of his Bishops.

	3	...	R×R
	4	R×R	P—R 4

Both Kt and Q are now *en prise* and Black threatens ... Q—Q 4; attacking both Knight and Rook and with a threat of mate.

	5	Q—Kt 3	Q—Q 7

The Knight is still safe from capture.

	6	R—K B 1	R—B 8
	7	B—Q 3	R×R *ch*
	8	B×R	Q—B 7

White was threatening Q—Kt 8 *ch*.

	9	Q—Kt 8 *ch*	B—B1
	10	Kt—B 7	

At last the Kt has moved away, but with a powerful threat.

	10	...	B—K 4
	11	Q×B *ch*	K—Kt 2
	12	Q—Q 7	Q×Kt
	13	Q×Q	B×Q
	14	B—Kt 5	B—Q 3
	15	B×P	B×R P

And the game is drawn. The struggle has, however, been keen and lively and White's combination was therefore justified.

4. COUNTER-ACTION

The term "even position" conjures up visions of dreary positions, dragging on interminably in expectation of some minute weakness or some big blunder. Quite the contrary can be the case, and then we see the art of chess at its highest. If in unequal positions we have seen counter-attacks produce play of the most exciting character, what can we expect when, in even positions, both players, in determined and whole-hearted fashion, attack each other to the utmost of their power? We have seen one example of this type and shall now examine one or two more. Without stopping to analyse positional manœuvres, with which we have now become familiar, we shall study cases in which both players simultaneously turn to direct action. This can happen in two ways —either the respective attacks may meet at the same point, or they may develop on opposite flanks. But when the battle rages over the whole range of the chessboard, what a feast for the spectator, and what an ordeal for the combatants !

It would not be correct to say that in all such cases the initial positions are even; only symmetrical positions are entirely even; but we are now only concerned with the actual struggle, and must overlook minute differences.

In Diag. 78 Black has a strong, supported, passed pawn. Unfortunately, it is blocked, and White can attack it as many times as it can be defended. In this case all the black pieces would be committed to the passive defence of this pawn, and White could break through with P—Q Kt 4. That is why it occurs to Black to advance his Q B P; the Q P is thereby weakened and White concentrates all his forces against it.

DIAGRAM 78

White: Duras; *Black:* Cohn
Carlsbad, 1911

1	...	Q—R 5
2	P—Kt 3	Q—R 4
3	K—Kt 2	P—B 5
4	Kt—B 4	Q—K 4
5	B × B	P—B 6
6	Q—Q 3	Kt × B
7	Kt—Q 5	

Threatening Kt—K 7 *ch*, as well as K R—Q 1, and
P—B 4. Black decides to force the advance of his pawn
by sacrificing the exchange.

7	...	R × Kt
8	P × R	Q × P
9	K R—Q 1	Kt—K 3

Protecting both the Q P as well as the Q B P, for if
White takes the Q B P, then, after the necessary
exchanges, P—B 7 wins.

10	Q × R P	R—R 1
11	Q—K 2	P—Q 6

With the Rooks threatening to occupy the seventh rank,

supported by the advanced pawns, Black now begins a
direct attack against the King.

12	R × Q P	Q—K Kt 4
13	Q—K 3	R × P *ch*
14	K—Kt 1	Q—K R 4
15	P—R 4	Q—K B 4

Threatening ... Q—R 6. If 16 P—K Kt 4, Q—B 5;
17 Q × Q, Kt × Q; with the threat of ... Kt—K 7 *ch.*

16	R (Q 3) × P	Q—R 6
17	R—B 8 *ch*	K—Kt 2

Black, thinking victory in sight, now makes a mistake:
with 17 ... Kt—B 1; he would probably have secured the
draw. After the text-move, White manages to assume
the offensive, without, however, neglecting his defence,
and so the final combination turns out well for him.

18	Q—K 5 *ch*	P—B 3
19	R (B 1)—B 7 *ch*	K—R 3
20	Q—K 3 *ch*	P—Kt 4
21	P × P *ch*	Kt × P

A little better would be: 21 ... P × P; 22 Q × Kt *ch*,
Q × Q; 23 R—B 6, and White has an extra pawn. But
he plays for a mate and—loses.

22	R × P *ch*	K × R
23	Q—K 7 *ch*	K—Kt 3
24	R—Kt 8 *ch*	K—B 4
25	R × Kt *ch*	and Black's Queen is lost.

In the next example (Diag. 79) White has a powerful
attack against the King, and as his Bishop is shut in, he
tries to free a diagonal for it. His own King is none
too secure, and he must conduct his attack cautiously
and with the greatest precision.

1	R—B 5	Q—B 6

If 1 ... P × R; 2 Kt × P *ch*, K—R 2; 3 Kt × R (R 6),

DIAGRAM 79

White: Duras; *Black:* Teichmann
Ostend, 1906

K × Kt; 4 Q—R 4 *ch*, K—Kt 2; 5 R—B 5, etc.

    2   P—K 5   P × P

Compulsory, because of P—K 6.

    3   R—Kt 5   K—R 2

Q—B 6 *ch* was threatened.

    4   Kt—B 5   P × Kt

—otherwise White would win the exchange. We see that White, by means of two sacrifices, has opened the diagonal for his Bishop.

    5   Q × P *ch*   R—Kt 3

If 5 ... K—R 1; 6 R—R 5.

    6   Q—B 6   Q—Q 5 *ch*
    7   R—B 2   Q—Q 8 *ch*
    8   K—R 2   P—K 5

By sacrificing the Rook, Black closes the Bishop's line and thus obtains a little freedom. A sacrifice helps him to pass from the defensive to the counter-attack.

    9   Q × R   R—R 3 *ch*
   10   K—Kt 3   Q—K 8

White threatened R × P *ch.* If 10 ... Q × P *ch*; 11 R—B 3, with the same threat.

11	Q × B	Q—K 6 *ch*
12	K—Kt 4	

White is not afraid to advance his King, as his attack is more potent than the enemy's threats.

12	...	P—B 4 *ch*
13	R (Kt 5) × P	R—Kt 3 *ch*

Threatening a mate in two, but—

14	Q × R *ch*

By a fresh sacrifice White at last seizes the initiative which is to decide the fate of the battle.

14	...	K × Q
15	R—B 6 *ch*	K—Kt 2
16	R—B 7 *ch*	K—Kt 1
17	R—B 8 *ch*	K—Kt 2
18	R (B 2)—B 7 *ch*	K—Kt 3
19	R—B 6 *ch*	K—Kt 2
20	R (B 8)—B 7 *ch*	K—Kt 1
21	K—R 5	

Excellent play. There is no defence against the threatened mate.

21	...	Q—K 7 *ch*
22	P—Kt 4	Resigns.

A game of chess can be very thrilling when played in this manner !

No less exciting is the following example (Diag. 80). Black, having sacrificed a pawn in the opening, has a splendid game. His Q B, on an open diagonal, prevents White from castling on the K side. He does his utmost to prevent him from castling on the other side as well. White, however, unwilling to submit to a passive defence,

DIAGRAM 80

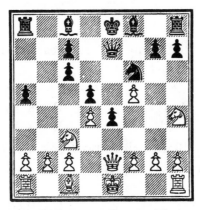

White: Pillsbury; *Black:* Tarrasch
Monte Carlo, 1903

conducts an active game and tries to increase his advantage in material.

1	B—Kt 5	B—R 3
2	B × Kt	Q × B
3	Q—R 5 *ch*	K—Q 2
4	Kt—Kt 6	

Practically forced: his Q P is attacked and ... B—K 2; attacking the Knight, is threatened.

4	...	Q × Q P

Black perseveres with the idea of keeping his King in the centre. His sacrifice of a Rook is less substantial than it looks, in view of the fact that both white Rooks are out of play.

5	Kt × R	B—B 4
6	Q—R 4	R × Kt
7	R—Q 1	Q—Kt 5

Threatening ... P—Q 5.

8	Q—Kt 4	K—Q 1

9	Q × Kt P	R—K 1
10	Q—B 6 *ch*	K—Q 2
11	P—Q R 3	

By releasing the Knight he threatens Kt × Q P, in
answer to ... Q × Kt P.

11	...	Q—Kt 3
12	R—Q 2	P—K 6
13	P × P	B × K P

In this way Black brings his Rook into the game and,
in effect, has an extra piece. White seeks salvation in
an attack.

14	Kt × P	B × R *db. ch*
15	K × B	Q—B 7 *ch*
16	K—Q 1	Q—K 7 *ch*
17	K—B 1	P × Kt
18	R—Q 1	

Again, as in the preceding game, White obtains the
initiative by sacrificing a piece. He has two pawns for
it and freedom of action.

18	...	P—B 3
19	Q—R 4	Q × P
20	Q × P *ch*	R—K 2
21	Q—R 4	Q—K 5
22	Q—R 8	Q × P
23	Q—R 8	B—B 1
24	Q—R 7 *ch*	K—K 1
25	Q × P	Q—B 5 *ch*
26	K—Kt 1	Q × P

And Black wins, having a Bishop for a pawn.

There could be no more fitting conclusion to this
book than these outstandingly beautiful examples of the
art of chess.

CONCLUSION

Our investigations are at an end; we have touched upon the most important types of positions and analysed their treatment. We have shown how to increase an advantage by exploiting enemy weaknesses whilst safeguarding the position.

The first edition of this book laid particular stress on the objective basis of our game—the three elements: space, time, and force—and we still insist on the necessity of giving them the most serious consideration. For one thing their importance is indisputable and we are never betrayed in trusting to their validity; in conforming to their principles we are banking on an unfailing certainty. Their neglect is the chief fault in the play of the average amateur; by becoming familiar with these principles he inevitably makes an important step forward in his playing strength.

But that is not enough. Chess is not a mechanical game; it appeals to and depends on the intellect. Therefore "ideas in chess" form the most important as well as the most interesting part of the game. That is why we play chess. For this reason the major portion of this book is devoted to "ideas in chess." Using technique as a starting point, we arrive, by the analysis of each position, at an understanding of its main idea, and of its distinctive features. This enables us to formulate a strategic plan. In carrying out this plan we must take advantage of any tactical possibility which may occur—that is how a chess player should think and act in the course of every game he plays.

Considerations of space have forced me to follow

rather general lines, without going into all details; these might well be treated in specialised monographs.

The most important examples given in the first edition have been retained, but many new ones taken from the very latest tournament practice have been added with the object of making this study of the middle game as complete and modern as possible.

A CATALOG OF SELECTED
DOVER BOOKS
IN ALL FIELDS OF INTEREST

A CATALOG OF SELECTED DOVER
BOOKS IN ALL FIELDS OF INTEREST

DRAWINGS OF REMBRANDT, edited by Seymour Slive. Updated Lippmann, Hofstede de Groot edition, with definitive scholarly apparatus. All portraits, biblical sketches, landscapes, nudes. Oriental figures, classical studies, together with selection of work by followers. 550 illustrations. Total of 630pp. 9⅛ × 12¼.
21485-0, 21486-9 Pa., Two-vol. set $29.90

GHOST AND HORROR STORIES OF AMBROSE BIERCE, Ambrose Bierce. 24 tales vividly imagined, strangely prophetic, and decades ahead of their time in technical skill: "The Damned Thing," "An Inhabitant of Carcosa," "The Eyes of the Panther," "Moxon's Master," and 20 more. 199pp. 5⅜ × 8½. 20767-6 Pa. $3.95

ETHICAL WRITINGS OF MAIMONIDES, Maimonides. Most significant ethical works of great medieval sage, newly translated for utmost precision, readability. Laws Concerning Character Traits, Eight Chapters, more. 192pp. 5⅜ × 8½.
24522-5 Pa. $4.50

THE EXPLORATION OF THE COLORADO RIVER AND ITS CANYONS, J. W. Powell. Full text of Powell's 1,000-mile expedition down the fabled Colorado in 1869. Superb account of terrain, geology, vegetation, Indians, famine, mutiny, treacherous rapids, mighty canyons, during exploration of last unknown part of continental U.S. 400pp. 5⅜ × 8½. 20094-9 Pa. $7.95

HISTORY OF PHILOSOPHY, Julián Marías. Clearest one-volume history on the market. Every major philosopher and dozens of others, to Existentialism and later. 505pp. 5⅜ × 8½. 21739-6 Pa. $9.95

ALL ABOUT LIGHTNING, Martin A. Uman. Highly readable non-technical survey of nature and causes of lightning, thunderstorms, ball lightning, St. Elmo's Fire, much more. Illustrated. 192pp. 5⅜ × 8½. 25237-X Pa. $5.95

SAILING ALONE AROUND THE WORLD, Captain Joshua Slocum. First man to sail around the world, alone, in small boat. One of great feats of seamanship told in delightful manner. 67 illustrations. 294pp. 5⅜ × 8½. 20326-3 Pa. $4.95

LETTERS AND NOTES ON THE MANNERS, CUSTOMS AND CONDITIONS OF THE NORTH AMERICAN INDIANS, George Catlin. Classic account of life among Plains Indians: ceremonies, hunt, warfare, etc. 312 plates. 572pp. of text. 6⅛ × 9¼. 22118-0, 22119-9, Pa. Two-vol. set $17.90

ALASKA: The Harriman Expedition, 1899, John Burroughs, John Muir, et al. Informative, engrossing accounts of two-month, 9,000-mile expedition. Native peoples, wildlife, forests, geography, salmon industry, glaciers, more. Profusely illustrated. 240 black-and-white line drawings. 124 black-and-white photographs. 3 maps. Index. 576pp. 5⅜ × 8½. 25109-8 Pa. $11.95

THE BOOK OF BEASTS: Being a Translation from a Latin Bestiary of the Twelfth Century, T. H. White. Wonderful catalog real and fanciful beasts: manticore, griffin, phoenix, amphivius, jaculus, many more. White's witty erudite commentary on scientific, historical aspects. Fascinating glimpse of medieval mind. Illustrated. 296pp. 5⅜ × 8¼. (Available in U.S. only) 24609-4 Pa. $6.95

FRANK LLOYD WRIGHT: ARCHITECTURE AND NATURE With 160 Illustrations, Donald Hoffmann. Profusely illustrated study of influence of nature—especially prairie—on Wright's designs for Fallingwater, Robie House, Guggenheim Museum, other masterpieces. 96pp. 9¼ × 10¾. 25098-9 Pa. $7.95

FRANK LLOYD WRIGHT'S FALLINGWATER, Donald Hoffmann. Wright's famous waterfall house: planning and construction of organic idea. History of site, owners, Wright's personal involvement. Photographs of various stages of building. Preface by Edgar Kaufmann, Jr. 100 illustrations. 112pp. 9¼ × 10. 23671-4 Pa. $8.95

YEARS WITH FRANK LLOYD WRIGHT: Apprentice to Genius, Edgar Tafel. Insightful memoir by a former apprentice presents a revealing portrait of Wright the man, the inspired teacher, the greatest American architect. 372 black-and-white illustrations. Preface. Index. vi + 228pp. 8¼ × 11. 24801-1 Pa. $10.95

THE STORY OF KING ARTHUR AND HIS KNIGHTS, Howard Pyle. Enchanting version of King Arthur fable has delighted generations with imaginative narratives of exciting adventures and unforgettable illustrations by the author. 41 illustrations. xviii + 313pp. 6⅛ × 9¼. 21445-1 Pa. $6.95

THE GODS OF THE EGYPTIANS, E. A. Wallis Budge. Thorough coverage of numerous gods of ancient Egypt by foremost Egyptologist. Information on evolution of cults, rites and gods; the cult of Osiris; the Book of the Dead and its rites; the sacred animals and birds; Heaven and Hell; and more. 956pp. 6⅛ × 9¼. 22055-9, 22056-7 Pa., Two-vol. set $21.90

A THEOLOGICO-POLITICAL TREATISE, Benedict Spinoza. Also contains unfinished *Political Treatise*. Great classic on religious liberty, theory of government on common consent. R. Elwes translation. Total of 421pp. 5⅜ × 8½. 20249-6 Pa. $6.95

INCIDENTS OF TRAVEL IN CENTRAL AMERICA, CHIAPAS, AND YUCATAN, John L. Stephens. Almost single-handed discovery of Maya culture; exploration of ruined cities, monuments, temples; customs of Indians. 115 drawings. 892pp. 5⅜ × 8½. 22404-X, 22405-8 Pa., Two-vol. set $15.90

LOS CAPRICHOS, Francisco Goya. 80 plates of wild, grotesque monsters and caricatures. Prado manuscript included. 183pp. 6⅜ × 9⅜. 22384-1 Pa. $5.95

AUTOBIOGRAPHY: The Story of My Experiments with Truth, Mohandas K. Gandhi. Not hagiography, but Gandhi in his own words. Boyhood, legal studies, purification, the growth of the Satyagraha (nonviolent protest) movement. Critical, inspiring work of the man who freed India. 480pp. 5⅜ × 8½. (Available in U.S. only) 24593-4 Pa. $6.95

ILLUSTRATED DICTIONARY OF HISTORIC ARCHITECTURE, edited by Cyril M. Harris. Extraordinary compendium of clear, concise definitions for over 5,000 important architectural terms complemented by over 2,000 line drawings. Covers full spectrum of architecture from ancient ruins to 20th-century Modernism. Preface. 592pp. 7½ × 9⅜. 24444-X Pa. $15.95

THE NIGHT BEFORE CHRISTMAS, Clement Moore. Full text, and woodcuts from original 1848 book. Also critical, historical material. 19 illustrations. 40pp. 4⅝ × 6. 22797-9 Pa. $2.50

THE LESSON OF JAPANESE ARCHITECTURE: 165 Photographs, Jiro Harada. Memorable gallery of 165 photographs taken in the 1930's of exquisite Japanese homes of the well-to-do and historic buildings. 13 line diagrams. 192pp. 8⅜ × 11¼. 24778-3 Pa. $10.95

THE AUTOBIOGRAPHY OF CHARLES DARWIN AND SELECTED LETTERS, edited by Francis Darwin. The fascinating life of eccentric genius composed of an intimate memoir by Darwin (intended for his children); commentary by his son, Francis; hundreds of fragments from notebooks, journals, papers; and letters to and from Lyell, Hooker, Huxley, Wallace and Henslow. xi + 365pp. 5⅜ × 8. 20479-0 Pa. $6.95

WONDERS OF THE SKY: Observing Rainbows, Comets, Eclipses, the Stars and Other Phenomena, Fred Schaaf. Charming, easy-to-read poetic guide to all manner of celestial events visible to the naked eye. Mock suns, glories, Belt of Venus, more. Illustrated. 299pp. 5¼ × 8¼. 24402-4 Pa. $7.95

BURNHAM'S CELESTIAL HANDBOOK, Robert Burnham, Jr. Thorough guide to the stars beyond our solar system. Exhaustive treatment. Alphabetical by constellation: Andromeda to Cetus in Vol. 1; Chamaeleon to Orion in Vol. 2; and Pavo to Vulpecula in Vol. 3. Hundreds of illustrations. Index in Vol. 3. 2,000pp. 6⅛ × 9¼. 23567-X, 23568-8, 23673-0 Pa., Three-vol. set $41.85

STAR NAMES: Their Lore and Meaning, Richard Hinckley Allen. Fascinating history of names various cultures have given to constellations and literary and folkloristic uses that have been made of stars. Indexes to subjects. Arabic and Greek names. Biblical references. Bibliography. 563pp. 5⅜ × 8½. 21079-0 Pa. $8.95

THIRTY YEARS THAT SHOOK PHYSICS: The Story of Quantum Theory, George Gamow. Lucid, accessible introduction to influential theory of energy and matter. Careful explanations of Dirac's anti-particles, Bohr's model of the atom, much more. 12 plates. Numerous drawings. 240pp. 5⅜ × 8½. 24895-X Pa. $5.95

CHINESE DOMESTIC FURNITURE IN PHOTOGRAPHS AND MEASURED DRAWINGS, Gustav Ecke. A rare volume, now affordably priced for antique collectors, furniture buffs and art historians. Detailed review of styles ranging from early Shang to late Ming. Unabridged republication. 161 black-and-white drawings, photos. Total of 224pp. 8⅜ × 11¼. (Available in U.S. only) 25171-3 Pa. $13.95

VINCENT VAN GOGH: A Biography, Julius Meier-Graefe. Dynamic, penetrating study of artist's life, relationship with brother, Theo, painting techniques, travels, more. Readable, engrossing. 160pp. 5⅜ × 8½. (Available in U.S. only) 25253-1 Pa. $4.95

HOW TO WRITE, Gertrude Stein. Gertrude Stein claimed anyone could understand her unconventional writing—here are clues to help. Fascinating improvisations, language experiments, explanations illuminate Stein's craft and the art of writing. Total of 414pp. 4⅝ × 6⅜. 23144-5 Pa. $6.95

ADVENTURES AT SEA IN THE GREAT AGE OF SAIL: Five Firsthand Narratives, edited by Elliot Snow. Rare true accounts of exploration, whaling, shipwreck, fierce natives, trade, shipboard life, more. 33 illustrations. Introduction. 353pp. 5⅜ × 8½. 25177-2 Pa. $8.95

THE HERBAL OR GENERAL HISTORY OF PLANTS, John Gerard. Classic descriptions of about 2,850 plants—with over 2,700 illustrations—includes Latin and English names, physical descriptions, varieties, time and place of growth, more. 2,706 illustrations. xlv + 1,678pp. 8½ × 12¼. 23147-X Cloth. $75.00

DOROTHY AND THE WIZARD IN OZ, L. Frank Baum. Dorothy and the Wizard visit the center of the Earth, where people are vegetables, glass houses grow and Oz characters reappear. Classic sequel to *Wizard of Oz*. 256pp. 5⅜ × 8. 24714-7 Pa. $5.95

SONGS OF EXPERIENCE: Facsimile Reproduction with 26 Plates in Full Color, William Blake. This facsimile of Blake's original "Illuminated Book" reproduces 26 full-color plates from a rare 1826 edition. Includes "The Tyger," "London," "Holy Thursday," and other immortal poems. 26 color plates. Printed text of poems. 48pp. 5¼ × 7. 24636-1 Pa. $3.50

SONGS OF INNOCENCE, William Blake. The first and most popular of Blake's famous "Illuminated Books," in a facsimile edition reproducing all 31 brightly colored plates. Additional printed text of each poem. 64pp. 5¼ × 7. 22764-2 Pa. $3.50

PRECIOUS STONES, Max Bauer. Classic, thorough study of diamonds, rubies, emeralds, garnets, etc.: physical character, occurrence, properties, use, similar topics. 20 plates, 8 in color. 94 figures. 659pp. 6⅛ × 9¼. 21910-0, 21911-9 Pa., Two-vol. set $15.90

ENCYCLOPEDIA OF VICTORIAN NEEDLEWORK, S. F. A. Caulfeild and Blanche Saward. Full, precise descriptions of stitches, techniques for dozens of needlecrafts—most exhaustive reference of its kind. Over 800 figures. Total of 679pp. 8⅛ × 11. Two volumes. Vol. 1 22800-2 Pa. $11.95
Vol. 2 22801-0 Pa. $11.95

THE MARVELOUS LAND OF OZ, L. Frank Baum. Second Oz book, the Scarecrow and Tin Woodman are back with hero named Tip, Oz magic. 136 illustrations. 287pp. 5⅜ × 8½. 20692-0 Pa. $5.95

WILD FOWL DECOYS, Joel Barber. Basic book on the subject, by foremost authority and collector. Reveals history of decoy making and rigging, place in American culture, different kinds of decoys, how to make them, and how to use them. 140 plates. 156pp. 7⅞ × 10¾. 20011-6 Pa. $8.95

HISTORY OF LACE, Mrs. Bury Palliser. Definitive, profusely illustrated chronicle of lace from earliest times to late 19th century. Laces of Italy, Greece, England, France, Belgium, etc. Landmark of needlework scholarship. 266 illustrations. 672pp. 6⅛ × 9¼. 24742-2 Pa. $14.95

ILLUSTRATED GUIDE TO SHAKER FURNITURE, Robert Meader. All furniture and appurtenances, with much on unknown local styles. 235 photos. 146pp. 9 × 12. 22819-3 Pa. $8.95

WHALE SHIPS AND WHALING: A Pictorial Survey, George Francis Dow. Over 200 vintage engravings, drawings, photographs of barks, brigs, cutters, other vessels. Also harpoons, lances, whaling guns, many other artifacts. Comprehensive text by foremost authority. 207 black-and-white illustrations. 288pp. 6 × 9. 24808-9 Pa. $8.95

THE BERTRAMS, Anthony Trollope. Powerful portrayal of blind self-will and thwarted ambition includes one of Trollope's most heartrending love stories. 497pp. 5⅜ × 8½. 25119-5 Pa. $9.95

ADVENTURES WITH A HAND LENS, Richard Headstrom. Clearly written guide to observing and studying flowers and grasses, fish scales, moth and insect wings, egg cases, buds, feathers, seeds, leaf scars, moss, molds, ferns, common crystals, etc.—all with an ordinary, inexpensive magnifying glass. 209 exact line drawings aid in your discoveries. 220pp. 5⅜ × 8½. 23330-8 Pa. $4.95

RODIN ON ART AND ARTISTS, Auguste Rodin. Great sculptor's candid, wide-ranging comments on meaning of art; great artists; relation of sculpture to poetry, painting, music; philosophy of life, more. 76 superb black-and-white illustrations of Rodin's sculpture, drawings and prints. 119pp. 8⅜ × 11¼. 24487-3 Pa. $7.95

FIFTY CLASSIC FRENCH FILMS, 1912–1982: A Pictorial Record, Anthony Slide. Memorable stills from Grand Illusion, Beauty and the Beast, Hiroshima, Mon Amour, many more. Credits, plot synopses, reviews, etc. 160pp. 8¼ × 11. 25256-6 Pa. $11.95

THE PRINCIPLES OF PSYCHOLOGY, William James. Famous long course complete, unabridged. Stream of thought, time perception, memory, experimental methods; great work decades ahead of its time. 94 figures. 1,391pp. 5⅜ × 8½. 20381-6, 20382-4 Pa., Two-vol. set $23.90

BODIES IN A BOOKSHOP, R. T. Campbell. Challenging mystery of blackmail and murder with ingenious plot and superbly drawn characters. In the best tradition of British suspense fiction. 192pp. 5⅜ × 8½. 24720-1 Pa. $3.95

CALLAS: PORTRAIT OF A PRIMA DONNA, George Jellinek. Renowned commentator on the musical scene chronicles incredible career and life of the most controversial, fascinating, influential operatic personality of our time. 64 black-and-white photographs. 416pp. 5⅜ × 8¼. 25047-4 Pa. $8.95

GEOMETRY, RELATIVITY AND THE FOURTH DIMENSION, Rudolph Rucker. Exposition of fourth dimension, concepts of relativity as Flatland characters continue adventures. Popular, easily followed yet accurate, profound. 141 illustrations. 133pp. 5⅜ × 8½. 23400-2 Pa. $4.95

HOUSEHOLD STORIES BY THE BROTHERS GRIMM, with pictures by Walter Crane. 53 classic stories—Rumpelstiltskin, Rapunzel, Hansel and Gretel, the Fisherman and his Wife, Snow White, Tom Thumb, Sleeping Beauty, Cinderella, and so much more—lavishly illustrated with original 19th century drawings. 114 illustrations. x + 269pp. 5⅜ × 8½. 21080-4 Pa. $4.95

SUNDIALS, Albert Waugh. Far and away the best, most thorough coverage of ideas, mathematics concerned, types, construction, adjusting anywhere. Over 100 illustrations. 230pp. 5⅜ × 8½. 22947-5 Pa. $4.95

PICTURE HISTORY OF THE NORMANDIE: With 190 Illustrations, Frank O. Braynard. Full story of legendary French ocean liner: Art Deco interiors, design innovations, furnishings, celebrities, maiden voyage, tragic fire, much more. Extensive text. 144pp. 8⅞ × 11¾. 25257-4 Pa. $10.95

THE FIRST AMERICAN COOKBOOK: A Facsimile of "American Cookery," 1796, Amelia Simmons. Facsimile of the first American-written cookbook published in the United States contains authentic recipes for colonial favorites—pumpkin pudding, winter squash pudding, spruce beer, Indian slapjacks, and more. Introductory Essay and Glossary of colonial cooking terms. 80pp. 5⅜ × 8½.
24710-4 Pa. $3.50

101 PUZZLES IN THOUGHT AND LOGIC, C. R. Wylie, Jr. Solve murders and robberies, find out which fishermen are liars, how a blind man could possibly identify a color—purely by your own reasoning! 107pp. 5⅜ × 8½. 20367-0 Pa. $2.50

THE BOOK OF WORLD-FAMOUS MUSIC—CLASSICAL, POPULAR AND FOLK, James J. Fuld. Revised and enlarged republication of landmark work in musico-bibliography. Full information about nearly 1,000 songs and compositions including first lines of music and lyrics. New supplement. Index. 800pp. 5⅜ × 8¼.
24857-7 Pa. $15.95

ANTHROPOLOGY AND MODERN LIFE, Franz Boas. Great anthropologist's classic treatise on race and culture. Introduction by Ruth Bunzel. Only inexpensive paperback edition. 255pp. 5⅜ × 8½. 25245-0 Pa. $6.95

THE TALE OF PETER RABBIT, Beatrix Potter. The inimitable Peter's terrifying adventure in Mr. McGregor's garden, with all 27 wonderful, full-color Potter illustrations. 55pp. 4¼ × 5½. (Available in U.S. only) 22827-4 Pa. $1.75

THREE PROPHETIC SCIENCE FICTION NOVELS, H. G. Wells. *When the Sleeper Wakes, A Story of the Days to Come* and *The Time Machine* (full version). 335pp. 5⅜ × 8½. (Available in U.S. only) 20605-X Pa. $6.95

APICIUS COOKERY AND DINING IN IMPERIAL ROME, edited and translated by Joseph Dommers Vehling. Oldest known cookbook in existence offers readers a clear picture of what foods Romans ate, how they prepared them, etc. 49 illustrations. 301pp. 6⅛ × 9¼. 23563-7 Pa. $7.95

SHAKESPEARE LEXICON AND QUOTATION DICTIONARY, Alexander Schmidt. Full definitions, locations, shades of meaning of every word in plays and poems. More than 50,000 exact quotations. 1,485pp. 6½ × 9¼.
22726-X, 22727-8 Pa., Two-vol. set $29.90

THE WORLD'S GREAT SPEECHES, edited by Lewis Copeland and Lawrence W. Lamm. Vast collection of 278 speeches from Greeks to 1970. Powerful and effective models; unique look at history. 842pp. 5⅜ × 8½. 20468-5 Pa. $11.95

THE BLUE FAIRY BOOK, Andrew Lang. The first, most famous collection, with many familiar tales: Little Red Riding Hood, Aladdin and the Wonderful Lamp, Puss in Boots, Sleeping Beauty, Hansel and Gretel, Rumpelstiltskin; 37 in all. 138 illustrations. 390pp. 5⅜ × 8½. 21437-0 Pa. $6.95

THE STORY OF THE CHAMPIONS OF THE ROUND TABLE, Howard Pyle. Sir Launcelot, Sir Tristram and Sir Percival in spirited adventures of love and triumph retold in Pyle's inimitable style. 50 drawings, 31 full-page. xviii + 329pp. 6½ × 9¼. 21883-X Pa. $7.95

AUDUBON AND HIS JOURNALS, Maria Audubon. Unmatched two-volume portrait of the great artist, naturalist and author contains his journals, an excellent biography by his granddaughter, expert annotations by the noted ornithologist, Dr. Elliott Coues, and 37 superb illustrations. Total of 1,200pp. 5⅜ × 8.
Vol. I 25143-8 Pa. $8.95
Vol. II 25144-6 Pa. $8.95

GREAT DINOSAUR HUNTERS AND THEIR DISCOVERIES, Edwin H. Colbert. Fascinating, lavishly illustrated chronicle of dinosaur research, 1820's to 1960. Achievements of Cope, Marsh, Brown, Buckland, Mantell, Huxley, many others. 384pp. 5¼ × 8¼. 24701-5 Pa. $7.95

THE TASTEMAKERS, Russell Lynes. Informal, illustrated social history of American taste 1850's–1950's. First popularized categories Highbrow, Lowbrow, Middlebrow. 129 illustrations. New (1979) afterword. 384pp. 6 × 9.
23993-4 Pa. $8.95

DOUBLE CROSS PURPOSES, Ronald A. Knox. A treasure hunt in the Scottish Highlands, an old map, unidentified corpse, surprise discoveries keep reader guessing in this cleverly intricate tale of financial skullduggery. 2 black-and-white maps. 320pp. 5⅜ × 8½. (Available in U.S. only) 25032-6 Pa. $6.95

AUTHENTIC VICTORIAN DECORATION AND ORNAMENTATION IN FULL COLOR: 46 Plates from "Studies in Design," Christopher Dresser. Superb full-color lithographs reproduced from rare original portfolio of a major Victorian designer. 48pp. 9¼ × 12¼. 25083-0 Pa. $7.95

PRIMITIVE ART, Franz Boas. Remains the best text ever prepared on subject, thoroughly discussing Indian, African, Asian, Australian, and, especially, Northern American primitive art. Over 950 illustrations show ceramics, masks, totem poles, weapons, textiles, paintings, much more. 376pp. 5⅜ × 8. 20025-6 Pa. $7.95

SIDELIGHTS ON RELATIVITY, Albert Einstein. Unabridged republication of two lectures delivered by the great physicist in 1920–21. *Ether and Relativity* and *Geometry and Experience.* Elegant ideas in non-mathematical form, accessible to intelligent layman. vi + 56pp. 5⅜ × 8½. 24511-X Pa. $2.95

THE WIT AND HUMOR OF OSCAR WILDE, edited by Alvin Redman. More than 1,000 ripostes, paradoxes, wisecracks: Work is the curse of the drinking classes, I can resist everything except temptation, etc. 258pp. 5⅜ × 8½. 20602-5 Pa. $4.95

ADVENTURES WITH A MICROSCOPE, Richard Headstrom. 59 adventures with clothing fibers, protozoa, ferns and lichens, roots and leaves, much more. 142 illustrations. 232pp. 5⅜ × 8½. 23471-1 Pa. $3.95

PLANTS OF THE BIBLE, Harold N. Moldenke and Alma L. Moldenke. Standard reference to all 230 plants mentioned in Scriptures. Latin name, biblical reference, uses, modern identity, much more. Unsurpassed encyclopedic resource for scholars, botanists, nature lovers, students of Bible. Bibliography. Indexes. 123 black-and-white illustrations. 384pp. 6 × 9. 25069-5 Pa. $8.95

FAMOUS AMERICAN WOMEN: A Biographical Dictionary from Colonial Times to the Present, Robert McHenry, ed. From Pocahontas to Rosa Parks, 1,035 distinguished American women documented in separate biographical entries. Accurate, up-to-date data, numerous categories, spans 400 years. Indices. 493pp. 6½ × 9¼. 24523-3 Pa. $10.95

THE FABULOUS INTERIORS OF THE GREAT OCEAN LINERS IN HISTORIC PHOTOGRAPHS, William H. Miller, Jr. Some 200 superb photographs capture exquisite interiors of world's great "floating palaces"—1890's to 1980's: *Titanic, Ile de France, Queen Elizabeth, United States, Europa,* more. Approx. 200 black-and-white photographs. Captions. Text. Introduction. 160pp. 8⅞ × 11¾. 24756-2 Pa. $9.95

THE GREAT LUXURY LINERS, 1927–1954: A Photographic Record, William H. Miller, Jr. Nostalgic tribute to heyday of ocean liners. 186 photos of Ile de France, Normandie, Leviathan, Queen Elizabeth, United States, many others. Interior and exterior views. Introduction. Captions. 160pp. 9 × 12. 24056-8 Pa. $10.95

A NATURAL HISTORY OF THE DUCKS, John Charles Phillips. Great landmark of ornithology offers complete detailed coverage of nearly 200 species and subspecies of ducks: gadwall, sheldrake, merganser, pintail, many more. 74 full-color plates, 102 black-and-white. Bibliography. Total of 1,920pp. 8⅝ × 11¼. 25141-1, 25142-X Cloth. Two-vol. set $100.00

THE SEAWEED HANDBOOK: An Illustrated Guide to Seaweeds from North Carolina to Canada, Thomas F. Lee. Concise reference covers 78 species. Scientific and common names, habitat, distribution, more. Finding keys for easy identification. 224pp. 5⅜ × 8½. 25215-9 Pa. $6.95

THE TEN BOOKS OF ARCHITECTURE: The 1755 Leoni Edition, Leon Battista Alberti. Rare classic helped introduce the glories of ancient architecture to the Renaissance. 68 black-and-white plates. 336pp. 8⅜ × 11¼. 25239-6 Pa. $14.95

MISS MACKENZIE, Anthony Trollope. Minor masterpieces by Victorian master unmasks many truths about life in 19th-century England. First inexpensive edition in years. 392pp. 5⅜ × 8½. 25201-9 Pa. $8.95

THE RIME OF THE ANCIENT MARINER, Gustave Doré, Samuel Taylor Coleridge. Dramatic engravings considered by many to be his greatest work. The terrifying space of the open sea, the storms and whirlpools of an unknown ocean, the ice of Antarctica, more—all rendered in a powerful, chilling manner. Full text. 38 plates. 77pp. 9¼ × 12. 22305-1 Pa. $4.95

THE EXPEDITIONS OF ZEBULON MONTGOMERY PIKE, Zebulon Montgomery Pike. Fascinating first-hand accounts (1805–6) of exploration of Mississippi River, Indian wars, capture by Spanish dragoons, much more. 1,088pp. 5⅜ × 8½. 25254-X, 25255-8 Pa. Two-vol. set $25.90

A CONCISE HISTORY OF PHOTOGRAPHY: Third Revised Edition, Helmut Gernsheim. Best one-volume history—camera obscura, photochemistry, daguerreotypes, evolution of cameras, film, more. Also artistic aspects—landscape, portraits, fine art, etc. 281 black-and-white photographs. 26 in color. 176pp. 8⅜ × 11¼. 25128-4 Pa. $13.95

THE DORÉ BIBLE ILLUSTRATIONS, Gustave Doré. 241 detailed plates from the Bible: the Creation scenes, Adam and Eve, Flood, Babylon, battle sequences, life of Jesus, etc. Each plate is accompanied by the verses from the King James version of the Bible. 241pp. 9 × 12. 23004-X Pa. $9.95

HUGGER-MUGGER IN THE LOUVRE, Elliot Paul. Second Homer Evans mystery-comedy. Theft at the Louvre involves sleuth in hilarious, madcap caper. "A knockout."—Books. 336pp. 5⅜ × 8½. 25185-3 Pa. $5.95

FLATLAND, E. A. Abbott. Intriguing and enormously popular science-fiction classic explores the complexities of trying to survive as a two-dimensional being in a three-dimensional world. Amusingly illustrated by the author. 16 illustrations. 103pp. 5⅜ × 8½. 20001-9 Pa. $2.50

THE HISTORY OF THE LEWIS AND CLARK EXPEDITION, Meriwether Lewis and William Clark, edited by Elliott Coues. Classic edition of Lewis and Clark's day-by-day journals that later became the basis for U.S. claims to Oregon and the West. Accurate and invaluable geographical, botanical, biological, meteorological and anthropological material. Total of 1,508pp. 5⅜ × 8½. 21268-8, 21269-6, 21270-X Pa. Three-vol. set $26.85

LANGUAGE, TRUTH AND LOGIC, Alfred J. Ayer. Famous, clear introduction to Vienna, Cambridge schools of Logical Positivism. Role of philosophy, elimination of metaphysics, nature of analysis, etc. 160pp. 5⅜ × 8½. (Available in U.S. and Canada only) 20010-8 Pa. $3.95

MATHEMATICS FOR THE NONMATHEMATICIAN, Morris Kline. Detailed, college-level treatment of mathematics in cultural and historical context, with numerous exercises. For liberal arts students. Preface. Recommended Reading Lists. Tables. Index. Numerous black-and-white figures. xvi + 641pp. 5⅜ × 8½. 24823-2 Pa. $11.95

HANDBOOK OF PICTORIAL SYMBOLS, Rudolph Modley. 3,250 signs and symbols, many systems in full; official or heavy commercial use. Arranged by subject. Most in Pictorial Archive series. 143pp. 8⅛ × 11. 23357-X Pa. $6.95

INCIDENTS OF TRAVEL IN YUCATAN, John L. Stephens. Classic (1843) exploration of jungles of Yucatan, looking for evidences of Maya civilization. Travel adventures, Mexican and Indian culture, etc. Total of 669pp. 5⅜ × 8½. 20926-1, 20927-X Pa., Two-vol. set $11.90

DEGAS: An Intimate Portrait, Ambroise Vollard. Charming, anecdotal memoir by famous art dealer of one of the greatest 19th-century French painters. 14 black-and-white illustrations. Introduction by Harold L. Van Doren. 96pp. 5⅜ × 8½.
25131-4 Pa. $4.95

PERSONAL NARRATIVE OF A PILGRIMAGE TO ALMANDINAH AND MECCAH, Richard Burton. Great travel classic by remarkably colorful personality. Burton, disguised as a Moroccan, visited sacred shrines of Islam, narrowly escaping death. 47 illustrations. 959pp. 5⅜ × 8½.   21217-3, 21218-1 Pa., Two-vol. set $19.90

PHRASE AND WORD ORIGINS, A. H. Holt. Entertaining, reliable, modern study of more than 1,200 colorful words, phrases, origins and histories. Much unexpected information. 254pp. 5⅜ × 8½.   20758-7 Pa. $5.95

THE RED THUMB MARK, R. Austin Freeman. In this first Dr. Thorndyke case, the great scientific detective draws fascinating conclusions from the nature of a single fingerprint. Exciting story, authentic science. 320pp. 5⅜ × 8½. (Available in U.S. only)   25210-8 Pa. $6.95

AN EGYPTIAN HIEROGLYPHIC DICTIONARY, E. A. Wallis Budge. Monumental work containing about 25,000 words or terms that occur in texts ranging from 3000 B.C. to 600 A.D. Each entry consists of a transliteration of the word, the word in hieroglyphs, and the meaning in English. 1,314pp. 6⅜ × 10.
23615-3, 23616-1 Pa., Two-vol. set $31.90

THE COMPLEAT STRATEGYST: Being a Primer on the Theory of Games of Strategy, J. D. Williams. Highly entertaining classic describes, with many illustrated examples, how to select best strategies in conflict situations. Prefaces. Appendices. xvi + 268pp. 5⅜ × 8½.   25101-2 Pa. $5.95

THE ROAD TO OZ, L. Frank Baum. Dorothy meets the Shaggy Man, little Button-Bright and the Rainbow's beautiful daughter in this delightful trip to the magical Land of Oz. 272pp. 5⅜ × 8.   25208-6 Pa. $5.95

POINT AND LINE TO PLANE, Wassily Kandinsky. Seminal exposition of role of point, line, other elements in non-objective painting. Essential to understanding 20th-century art. 127 illustrations. 192pp. 6½ × 9¼.   23808-3 Pa. $5.95

LADY ANNA, Anthony Trollope. Moving chronicle of Countess Lovel's bitter struggle to win for herself and daughter Anna their rightful rank and fortune—perhaps at cost of sanity itself. 384pp. 5⅜ × 8½.   24669-8 Pa. $8.95

EGYPTIAN MAGIC, E. A. Wallis Budge. Sums up all that is known about magic in Ancient Egypt: the role of magic in controlling the gods, powerful amulets that warded off evil spirits, scarabs of immortality, use of wax images, formulas and spells, the secret name, much more. 253pp. 5⅜ × 8½.   22681-6 Pa. $4.50

THE DANCE OF SIVA, Ananda Coomaraswamy. Preeminent authority unfolds the vast metaphysic of India: the revelation of her art, conception of the universe, social organization, etc. 27 reproductions of art masterpieces. 192pp. 5⅜ × 8½.
24817-8 Pa. $5.95

CHRISTMAS CUSTOMS AND TRADITIONS, Clement A. Miles. Origin, evolution, significance of religious, secular practices. Caroling, gifts, yule logs, much more. Full, scholarly yet fascinating; non-sectarian. 400pp. 5⅜ × 8½.
23354-5 Pa. $6.95

THE HUMAN FIGURE IN MOTION, Eadweard Muybridge. More than 4,500 stopped-action photos, in action series, showing undraped men, women, children jumping, lying down, throwing, sitting, wrestling, carrying, etc. 390pp. 7⅞ × 10⅝.
20204-6 Cloth. $21.95

THE MAN WHO WAS THURSDAY, Gilbert Keith Chesterton. Witty, fast-paced novel about a club of anarchists in turn-of-the-century London. Brilliant social, religious, philosophical speculations. 128pp. 5⅜ × 8½.
25121-7 Pa. $3.95

A CEZANNE SKETCHBOOK: Figures, Portraits, Landscapes and Still Lifes, Paul Cezanne. Great artist experiments with tonal effects, light, mass, other qualities in over 100 drawings. A revealing view of developing master painter, precursor of Cubism. 102 black-and-white illustrations. 144pp. 8¾ × 6⅝.
24790-2 Pa. $5.95

AN ENCYCLOPEDIA OF BATTLES: Accounts of Over 1,560 Battles from 1479 B.C. to the Present, David Eggenberger. Presents essential details of every major battle in recorded history, from the first battle of Megiddo in 1479 B.C. to Grenada in 1984. List of Battle Maps. New Appendix covering the years 1967–1984. Index. 99 illustrations. 544pp. 6½ × 9¼.
24913-1 Pa. $14.95

AN ETYMOLOGICAL DICTIONARY OF MODERN ENGLISH, Ernest Weekley. Richest, fullest work, by foremost British lexicographer. Detailed word histories. Inexhaustible. Total of 856pp. 6½ × 9¼.
21873-2, 21874-0 Pa., Two-vol. set $17.00

WEBSTER'S AMERICAN MILITARY BIOGRAPHIES, edited by Robert McHenry. Over 1,000 figures who shaped 3 centuries of American military history. Detailed biographies of Nathan Hale, Douglas MacArthur, Mary Hallaren, others. Chronologies of engagements, more. Introduction. Addenda. 1,033 entries in alphabetical order. xi + 548pp. 6½ × 9¼. (Available in U.S. only)
24758-9 Pa. $13.95

LIFE IN ANCIENT EGYPT, Adolf Erman. Detailed older account, with much not in more recent books: domestic life, religion, magic, medicine, commerce, and whatever else needed for complete picture. Many illustrations. 597pp. 5⅜ × 8½.
22632-8 Pa. $8.95

HISTORIC COSTUME IN PICTURES, Braun & Schneider. Over 1,450 costumed figures shown, covering a wide variety of peoples: kings, emperors, nobles, priests, servants, soldiers, scholars, townsfolk, peasants, merchants, courtiers, cavaliers, and more. 256pp. 8⅜ × 11¼.
23150-X Pa. $9.95

THE NOTEBOOKS OF LEONARDO DA VINCI, edited by J. P. Richter. Extracts from manuscripts reveal great genius; on painting, sculpture, anatomy, sciences, geography, etc. Both Italian and English. 186 ms. pages reproduced, plus 500 additional drawings, including studies for *Last Supper*, *Sforza* monument, etc. 860pp. 7⅞ × 10¾. (Available in U.S. only) 22572-0, 22573-9 Pa., Two-vol. set $31.90

THE ART NOUVEAU STYLE BOOK OF ALPHONSE MUCHA: All 72 Plates from "Documents Decoratifs" in Original Color, Alphonse Mucha. Rare copyright-free design portfolio by high priest of Art Nouveau. Jewelry, wallpaper, stained glass, furniture, figure studies, plant and animal motifs, etc. Only complete one-volume edition. 80pp. 9⅜ × 12¼. 24044-4 Pa. $9.95

ANIMALS: 1,419 COPYRIGHT-FREE ILLUSTRATIONS OF MAMMALS, BIRDS, FISH, INSECTS, ETC., edited by Jim Harter. Clear wood engravings present, in extremely lifelike poses, over 1,000 species of animals. One of the most extensive pictorial sourcebooks of its kind. Captions. Index. 284pp. 9 × 12. 23766-4 Pa. $9.95

OBELISTS FLY HIGH, C. Daly King. Masterpiece of American detective fiction, long out of print, involves murder on a 1935 transcontinental flight—"a very thrilling story"—NY Times. Unabridged and unaltered republication of the edition published by William Collins Sons & Co. Ltd., London, 1935. 288pp. 5⅜ × 8½. (Available in U.S. only) 25036-9 Pa. $5.95

VICTORIAN AND EDWARDIAN FASHION: A Photographic Survey, Alison Gernsheim. First fashion history completely illustrated by contemporary photographs. Full text plus 235 photos, 1840–1914, in which many celebrities appear. 240pp. 6½ × 9¼. 24205-6 Pa. $6.95

THE ART OF THE FRENCH ILLUSTRATED BOOK, 1700–1914, Gordon N. Ray. Over 630 superb book illustrations by Fragonard, Delacroix, Daumier, Doré, Grandville, Manet, Mucha, Steinlen, Toulouse-Lautrec and many others. Preface. Introduction. 633 halftones. Indices of artists, authors & titles, binders and provenances. Appendices. Bibliography. 608pp. 8⅜ × 11¼. 25086-5 Pa. $24.95

THE WONDERFUL WIZARD OF OZ, L. Frank Baum. Facsimile in full color of America's finest children's classic. 143 illustrations by W. W. Denslow. 267pp. 5⅜ × 8½. 20691-2 Pa. $7.95

FRONTIERS OF MODERN PHYSICS: New Perspectives on Cosmology, Relativity, Black Holes and Extraterrestrial Intelligence, Tony Rothman, et al. For the intelligent layman. Subjects include: cosmological models of the universe; black holes; the neutrino; the search for extraterrestrial intelligence. Introduction. 46 black-and-white illustrations. 192pp. 5⅜ × 8½. 24587-X Pa. $7.95

THE FRIENDLY STARS, Martha Evans Martin & Donald Howard Menzel. Classic text marshalls the stars together in an engaging, non-technical survey, presenting them as sources of beauty in night sky. 23 illustrations. Foreword. 2 star charts. Index. 147pp. 5⅜ × 8½. 21099-5 Pa. $3.95

FADS AND FALLACIES IN THE NAME OF SCIENCE, Martin Gardner. Fair, witty appraisal of cranks, quacks, and quackeries of science and pseudoscience: hollow earth, Velikovsky, orgone energy, Dianetics, flying saucers, Bridey Murphy, food and medical fads, etc. Revised, expanded In the Name of Science. "A very able and even-tempered presentation."—The New Yorker. 363pp. 5⅜ × 8.

20394-8 Pa. $6.95

ANCIENT EGYPT: ITS CULTURE AND HISTORY, J. E Manchip White. From pre-dynastics through Ptolemies: society, history, political structure, religion, daily life, literature, cultural heritage. 48 plates. 217pp. 5⅜ × 8½. 22548-8 Pa. $5.95

CATALOG OF DOVER BOOKS

SIR HARRY HOTSPUR OF HUMBLETHWAITE, Anthony Trollope. Incisive, unconventional psychological study of a conflict between a wealthy baronet, his idealistic daughter, and their scapegrace cousin. The 1870 novel in its first inexpensive edition in years. 250pp. 5⅜ × 8½. 24953-0 Pa. $5.95

LASERS AND HOLOGRAPHY, Winston E. Kock. Sound introduction to burgeoning field, expanded (1981) for second edition. Wave patterns, coherence, lasers, diffraction, zone plates, properties of holograms, recent advances. 84 illustrations. 160pp. 5⅜ × 8¼. (Except in United Kingdom) 24041-X Pa. $3.95

INTRODUCTION TO ARTIFICIAL INTELLIGENCE: SECOND, EN-LARGED EDITION, Philip C. Jackson, Jr. Comprehensive survey of artificial intelligence—the study of how machines (computers) can be made to act intelligently. Includes introductory and advanced material. Extensive notes updating the main text. 132 black-and-white illustrations. 512pp. 5⅜ × 8½. 24864-X Pa. $8.95

HISTORY OF INDIAN AND INDONESIAN ART, Ananda K. Coomaraswamy. Over 400 illustrations illuminate classic study of Indian art from earliest Harappa finds to early 20th century. Provides philosophical, religious and social insights. 304pp. 6⅜ × 9⅜. 25005-9 Pa. $9.95

THE GOLEM, Gustav Meyrink. Most famous supernatural novel in modern European literature, set in Ghetto of Old Prague around 1890. Compelling story of mystical experiences, strange transformations, profound terror. 13 black-and-white illustrations. 224pp. 5⅜ × 8½. (Available in U.S. only) 25025-3 Pa. $6.95

PICTORIAL ENCYCLOPEDIA OF HISTORIC ARCHITECTURAL PLANS, DETAILS AND ELEMENTS: With 1,880 Line Drawings of Arches, Domes, Doorways, Facades, Gables, Windows, etc., John Theodore Haneman. Sourcebook of inspiration for architects, designers, others. Bibliography. Captions. 141pp. 9 × 12. 24605-1 Pa. $7.95

BENCHLEY LOST AND FOUND, Robert Benchley. Finest humor from early 30's, about pet peeves, child psychologists, post office and others. Mostly unavailable elsewhere. 73 illustrations by Peter Arno and others. 183pp. 5⅜ × 8½. 22410-4 Pa. $4.95

ERTÉ GRAPHICS, Erté. Collection of striking color graphics: *Seasons, Alphabet, Numerals, Aces* and *Precious Stones.* 50 plates, including 4 on covers. 48pp. 9⅜ × 12¼. 23580-7 Pa. $7.95

THE JOURNAL OF HENRY D. THOREAU, edited by Bradford Torrey, F. H. Allen. Complete reprinting of 14 volumes, 1837–61, over two million words; the sourcebooks for *Walden,* etc. Definitive. All original sketches, plus 75 photographs. 1,804pp. 8½ × 12¼. 20312-3, 20313-1 Cloth., Two-vol. set $120.00

CASTLES: THEIR CONSTRUCTION AND HISTORY, Sidney Toy. Traces castle development from ancient roots. Nearly 200 photographs and drawings illustrate moats, keeps, baileys, many other features. Caernarvon, Dover Castles, Hadrian's Wall, Tower of London, dozens more. 256pp. 5⅜ × 8¼. 24898-4 Pa. $6.95

CATALOG OF DOVER BOOKS

AMERICAN CLIPPER SHIPS: 1833–1858, Octavius T. Howe & Frederick C. Matthews. Fully-illustrated, encyclopedic review of 352 clipper ships from the period of America's greatest maritime supremacy. Introduction. 109 halftones. 5 black-and-white line illustrations. Index. Total of 928pp. 5⅜ × 8½.
25115-2, 25116-0 Pa., Two-vol. set $17.90

TOWARDS A NEW ARCHITECTURE, Le Corbusier. Pioneering manifesto by great architect, near legendary founder of "International School." Technical and aesthetic theories, views on industry, economics, relation of form to function, "mass-production spirit," much more. Profusely illustrated. Unabridged translation of 13th French edition. Introduction by Frederick Etchells. 320pp. 6⅛ × 9¼. (Available in U.S. only)
25023-7 Pa. $8.95

THE BOOK OF KELLS, edited by Blanche Cirker. Inexpensive collection of 32 full-color, full-page plates from the greatest illuminated manuscript of the Middle Ages, painstakingly reproduced from rare facsimile edition. Publisher's Note. Captions. 32pp. 9⅜ × 12¼.
24345-1 Pa. $4.95

BEST SCIENCE FICTION STORIES OF H. G. WELLS, H. G. Wells. Full novel *The Invisible Man,* plus 17 short stories: "The Crystal Egg," "Aepyornis Island," "The Strange Orchid," etc. 303pp. 5⅜ × 8½. (Available in U.S. only)
21531-8 Pa. $6.95

AMERICAN SAILING SHIPS: Their Plans and History, Charles G. Davis. Photos, construction details of schooners, frigates, clippers, other sailcraft of 18th to early 20th centuries—plus entertaining discourse on design, rigging, nautical lore, much more. 137 black-and-white illustrations. 240pp. 6⅛ × 9¼.
24658-2 Pa. $6.95

ENTERTAINING MATHEMATICAL PUZZLES, Martin Gardner. Selection of author's favorite conundrums involving arithmetic, money, speed, etc., with lively commentary. Complete solutions. 112pp. 5⅜ × 8½.
25211-6 Pa. $2.95

THE WILL TO BELIEVE, HUMAN IMMORTALITY, William James. Two books bound together. Effect of irrational on logical, and arguments for human immortality. 402pp. 5⅜ × 8½.
20291-7 Pa. $7.95

THE HAUNTED MONASTERY and THE CHINESE MAZE MURDERS, Robert Van Gulik. 2 full novels by Van Gulik continue adventures of Judge Dee and his companions. An evil Taoist monastery, seemingly supernatural events; overgrown topiary maze that hides strange crimes. Set in 7th-century China. 27 illustrations. 328pp. 5⅜ × 8½.
23502-5 Pa. $6.95

CELEBRATED CASES OF JUDGE DEE (DEE GOONG AN), translated by Robert Van Gulik. Authentic 18th-century Chinese detective novel; Dee and associates solve three interlocked cases. Led to Van Gulik's own stories with same characters. Extensive introduction. 9 illustrations. 237pp. 5⅜ × 8½.
23337-5 Pa. $4.95

Prices subject to change without notice.
Available at your book dealer or write for free catalog to Dept. GI, Dover Publications, Inc., 31 East 2nd St., Mineola, N.Y. 11501. Dover publishes more than 175 books each year on science, elementary and advanced mathematics, biology, music, art, literary history, social sciences and other areas.